# GROUND COVER PLANTS

■ Step by Step to Growing Success ■

## Stephen Taffler

CROWOOD GARDENING GUIDES

First published in 1991 by
The Crowood Press Ltd
Ramsbury, Marlborough,
Wiltshire SN8 2HR

**British Library Cataloguing in Publication Data**

Taffler, Stephen
  Ground cover plants
  I. Plants
  I. Title
  635.964

ISBN 1 85223 207 2

**Acknowledgements**
Photographs by Stephen Taffler
Line-drawings by Claire Upsdale-Jones

**Dedication**  I dedicate this book to my eldest son, Simon, who has gained
some knowledge of plants through being, in his youth, my attendant helper
with garden chores, pot boy and main assistant in controlling unwanted
weeds amongst my treasured plants. I would like to think that it was through
this experience of being with me in the garden, seeing plants close to, study-
ing their growth habits and enjoying this interest, that he is now a firm
believer in the use of plants for health and healing and is a practitioner in
alternative and complementary medicine.

  I wish to record my gratitude to my wife Gill, for her patience and
understanding, help and advice in preparing the manuscript. This, despite her
apprehension in having to come to terms with new technology with our recent acquisition of a word processor, something that seems to come as second nature to every young person who is already so familiar with any
electronic wizardry, be it calculator or computer.

  I am very grateful for the help and assistance, so freely given, in the writing
of this book, by my many friends in the horticultural world.

Typeset by Avonset, Midsomer Norton, Bath
Printed and bound by Times Publishing Group, Singapore

# Contents

# Preface

As with my first book *Climbing Plants and Wall Shrubs* in this excellent Crowood Gardening Guide series, I have endeavoured to make this book 'user friendly'. The plants mentioned are a selection of worthwhile plants suitable for ground cover, most of which I have grown successfully over a long period, though it is fair to state these were in gardens situated in the middle to southern parts of England.

The cultivation of these plants is relatively easy if the simple guide-lines suggested are followed. I would also like to recommend the reading of a companion book in this series, *Garden Design* by Brian Leverett. I feel that many readers, who are wanting to scrap and start again with their gardens or parts of gardens or just to build new pathways or other hard landscape structures, will find helpful good advice contained therein and to which my book *Ground Cover Plants* is complementary.

*Fig 1  Trillium sessile (wake robin). A clump forming perennial planted in dappled shade. An effective, seasonal, ground cover.*

# Introduction

Our gardens are the settings for our houses and as such should be planted with the same care given to the furnishing of the home.

Ground cover plants can be chosen for every possible site so that the covering of the ground and the filling of the garden with beauty is possible, no matter what the soil, climate or aspect.

Each garden is completely different from the next and no general rule can be laid down about the way in which it should be planted. Let your plants do much of the routine chores; instead of weeding, let your plants suppress the weeds. Remember that there may come a time when you will prefer to sit back rather than spend your time bending or stooping. In this instance, the garden may become a source of anxiety and responsibility rather than a recreation and a pleasure.

In many parts of the garden, it is possible to

*Fig 2   Looking through to a sunlit garden.*

Fig 3 *The annual Tropaeolum 'Alaska' has attractive variegated leaves and bright orange flowers. Seeds should be saved to provide plants for the following season.*

create by foliage and form alone, colourful and interesting planting. If properly chosen and given a little care, ground cover plants rank along with mulches as the greatest labour-saving moisture savers in the contemporary garden.

These plants can have leaves in many shades of green, they can be shiny or matt, simple or intricately serrated and some can be selected for the colour or variegation in their leaves. Those plants that are evergreen provide all-year-round cover, and some will give autumn tints or provide seasonal colour with their flowers.

These different shapes, textures and colours of foliage and flower will ensure that your plantings will never look monotonous. By carefully positioning adjacent plants so that they contrast with or complement each other, a palette of colour

will be created that will give endless interest and pleasure. Choose under-planting to contrast with the trees, shrubs and taller plants with which they are to be used. A silver carpet is effective under red-leaved shrubs, glaucous plants look well against dark green, golden foliage can be used where a suggestion of sunshine and light is needed. In a shady part of the garden, the splashes of colour that variegated foliage will provide can be quite dramatic. An excellent and gentle picture can be created by mixing greys, soft greens and bluish foliage.

Consider realistically how much time you are willing to spend on maintenance. Some garden designs and plantings will be more time consuming than others. If time is limited, plant your garden with trees, shrubs and *ground cover*.

# CHAPTER 1

# Gardens and Gardening

Many of us have romantic ideas about how we would like our gardens to look. Some imagine that they would like the tranquil, colourful cottage garden where the plants intermingle and so weave a pattern for a colourful display around the thatched cottage. Unfortunately, many of us live with suburban gardens with the squareness of fences and the sharp corners of modern brick houses.

In reality, the cottage of yester-year was really a smallholding where the cottager grew sustenance for the kitchen table. In the main, these cottages housed low-paid workers, labourers, self-employed thatchers, craft workers, weavers

*Fig 4   A well-graded planting with* Diascia, Antholyza, Phlox *'Norah Leigh' and red and blue salvias.*

*Fig 5  A good example of a well-filled border at Jenkyn Place, Hampshire.*

or potters and so on. To feed the family and subsidize a low income, they kept pigs, goats, geese, chickens and bees and grew fruit, vegetables and herbs. Their gardens also provided the ingredients for wine, medicines and household requisites. Any part of the garden that was decorative would almost invariably be at the front of the cottage which led off from a lane. Such a garden was very often composed of a carpet of invasive species of plants left to get on with growing as best they could. Such spreads of old-fashioned plants and flowers in full bloom are those that are portrayed today in our contemporary glossy and gardening magazines.

Today, we have available a much wider range of plant varieties and cultivars than had the cottage gardens of yesterday. Gardeners today enjoy swapping plants, seeds and cuttings and there are plenty of nurseries and garden centres for us to visit where we can purchase plants as we please. There are many specialist plant societies and most gardeners are happy to share their knowledge with fellow enthusiasts. They visit each other's gardens and compare notes and take advantage of the many open days organized by the specialist societies.

Very few people reading this book will be professional landscapers who specialize in style. It is more likely to be read by the enthusiasts who have discovered over the years, by trial and error, what works and what does not. It is by looking at successful gardens, observing how plants have been arranged and talking to the owners, that we learn about their successes and failures. It is a good idea to take notes and build up a fund of knowledge from other people's experiences.

Each garden is different and when making a

selection of ground cover plants (or any type of plant) for a particular site it is necessary to give consideration to the conditions under which the plants are to be grown. Selection will need to be made on the basis of preference for or tolerance of sun or shade, wet or dry conditions, clay, chalk or acid soils.

As parts of the garden will have differing micro-climates, in all probability due to man-made structures such as walls, paths, patios and ter-races, so the make up of the soil may differ from area to area within the boundary of your garden. In a small garden, surprisingly, there can be quite a variation in these microclimates. Some parts of the garden will have morning sun, some parts the evening sun and some gardens will have sun all day long. These variations, together with the amount of rainfall, frost and wind and the actual make up of the soil, have to be borne in mind when plants are being selected for particular areas.

One can choose plants that relish sunshine and those that grow best in the shade. Similarly, wind tolerant plants can be chosen and those that are frost tolerant will need to be chosen by those of you who garden in exposed areas or frost hollows and in the north of Britain or in the colder climes of some European countries.

Ground cover plants can be obtained in a wide range of leaf shapes, textures and colours, they can be evergreen, woody or herbaceous. A good ground cover plant needs to be of a low-growing, spreading habit and one which will quickly provide a sufficiently dense cover with foliage or twiggy growth to suppress germination and development of bird- or wind-carried weed seeds, thus eliminating the need for continual weed-control measures in the planted area.

*Fig 6* Heuchera micrantha *'Palace Purple', a clump former in the purple-leaved range.*

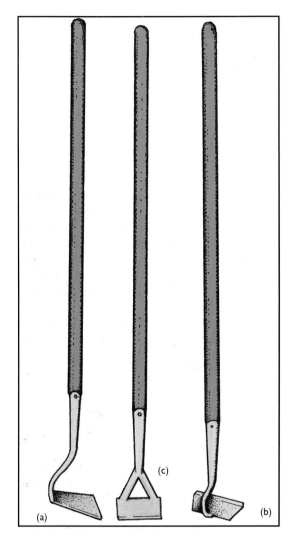

Fig 8   A close-up of the leaves of Elaeagnus pungens 'Dicksonii'.

Fig 7   Hand weeding tools: (a) a swoe;
(b) a draw hoe; (c) a Dutch hoe.

Whatever plants are selected, it is essential to thoroughly clean the area to be planted from all traces of perennial weeds and, if time allows, to cultivate the soil at intervals, to induce germination of any annual or perennial weed seed. The weed seedlings can then be destroyed by hoeing or by a contact weed-killer before planting commences.

Fig 8a   A border of mixed planting providing excellent ground cover.

CHAPTER 2

# Living Carpets of Ground Cover

There are many circumstances where there is a need to have certain areas in the garden covered with weed suppressing plants. Fairly large areas can be made attractive all year round after the initial effort has been made to clear the ground of all annual and perennial weeds. Many ground cover plants thrive under difficult growing condi-tions, give a natural beauty for very little cost and will virtually take care of themselves.

Ground cover is the gardening technique by which plants are grown close together so that their continuous canopy of leaves over the soil will grow thickly enough to inhibit weed growth. This weed growth fails through lack of light, and

*Fig 9* Tolmiea menziesii *'Taff's Gold', the pick-a-back plant, makes a superb, bright, weed suppressor.*

Fig 10   A trial ground effect of summer bedding plants. A very labour-intensive and seasonal
planting. Most colourful, but hardly my interpretation of 'low maintenance' ground cover.

reduced ability to manufacture the starches and
sugars necessary for growth and survival. We can
see nature practising this habit in the wild where
plants that are most suited to a particular soil and
site survive and flourish, smothering the weaker
plants.

## The Ideal Garden

All cultivation of garden plants is aimed at main-
taining those plants of your choice in a man-made
environment. It is the gardener who chooses
what is to grow and survive. These 'living
carpets' of ground cover plants cut down the
hours spent on hand weeding and the laborious
hoeing that is necessary for the neat and tidy
cultivation of 'bare soil' gardening. Surely, the
ideal garden for most of us is one that gives

pleasure with a long display of colour and the
minimum of work.

Ground cover is helpful for those starting new
gardens and is ideal for older people who may be
finding that their gardens are becoming too
labour intensive. Plantings like these are becoming increasingly popular with professional gardeners, landscape architects, garden designers
and those who manage and care for our national
heritage gardens.

Unfortunately, the tradition of training with its
encumbent hierarchy of head gardener down to
pot boy has almost disappeared to the point that
knowledgeable labour is not available for hire,
either for the householder or for those with
large estates.

Ground cover plants are likely to be perennial,
relatively low growing and of a spreading habit.

They must be able to thrive with the minimum of maintenance and be hardy enough for the area where they are to grow. Their leaf colour may change seasonally and they can have, as a bonus, attractive and colourful flowers.

Plants and shrubs that are evergreen will always provide the background for other plantings. After all, green is a colour of many shades and it is the most important colour in a garden. It is with us for possibly the longest in the gardening year and without it, the garden would look dull, dreary and barren, an almost unthinkable state of affairs.

I hope that I will persuade some gardeners who think mainly in terms of flowers, that there is beauty and interest in the other parts of a plant. Consider the fact that foliage lasts longer in the garden than do most flowers and coloured foliage can very often have much the same

*Fig II* Euonymus fortunei *'Emerald Gaiety'.*

*Fig 12* Stachys lanata *(lamb's ears) with lovely, silver-felted leaves.*

visual impact and appeal. Silver foliage plants are numerous and have a delicacy and lightness that adds to the variety of leaf colour. There are many marvellous plants in circulation in this country, so try to aim for a garden that can offer something to admire every day of the year.

I have searched through dictionaries and many gardening books to find a concise definition of what is meant by ground cover, in the horticultural sense, but to no avail. I therefore offer the following interpretation: ground cover — hence ground cover plants — are those plants that are close growing and wide spreading and essentially non-invasive. They can be clump forming and are often both durable and attractive. The plants knit together to form a dense and

Fig 13  A massed herbaceous planting with Buphthalmum and Matricaria, the pink flowers are from a Malva and a superb stand of Phlox 'Harlequin'. An example of planting to be emulated.

varied cover for the soil, thereby suppressing weeds and conserving moisture. This minimizes the necessity for hand weeding and maintenance with the hoe. They can be chosen to give a natural beauty for very little cost.

There is, unfortunately, no true dividing line between those plants that are good as ground cover and those that are not. The success of the chosen ground cover plants depends much upon the environment and the selection of the most suitable plants for these conditions by the

gardener. For the beginner, it is as well to start with those plants that are easy to establish and will continue to grow vigorously, even though they might well need to be restrained at a later date.

Always consider the scale and size of your garden and select ground cover plants that will grow to the size and height appropriate to the garden. Those with small city gardens will no doubt have to choose small, clump forming plants for their ground cover as will those with small suburban gardens. However, those of you with larger gardens can experiment with massed plantings of one or two specific plants to create the desired effect. This type of planting can be very restful on the eye and will act as a relief to the bolder, taller, herbaceous plants, flowering trees and shrubs. Try to grade your plantings from the rear of beds which often house low-growing trees and shrubs, through to tall, herbaceous flowering perennials to a foreground of low-maintenance ground cover.

However, for the plant collector, like myself, such an arrangement is just not practical. I have to content myself with growing plants in less than ideal juxtaposition as my acquisitive nature impels me to collect more and more interesting plants. Plants seem to do better when growing close to their neighbours rather than in isolation.

## Preparing the Ground

Whilst preparing the soil for planting, mulching and enriching with compost or fertilizers, give your back a break and some relief from digging and weeding with its consequent continual bending. Do visit, in any season, public parks and gardens, take a notebook with you and record those plants that you like and would wish to obtain. Take advantage of those gardens that have open days. In Britain these are well publicized in garden magazines, newspapers and of course, the 'Yellow Book', *Gardens in England and Wales Open to the Public*. This book is published annually by The National Gardens Scheme.

Remember it is wise before making any selection of plants, to study their attributes and limitations. It is important to find the right plants for every position in your garden; there are innumerable plants from which to choose to enjoy ground cover. I am sure most readers would agree that a garden well clothed is more pleasing than one in which there are expanses of bare ground.

You may have a limited budget with which to purchase plants so try to propagate plants that you have already purchased or that are already in

Fig 14 *The golden, finely cut leaves of* Sambucus racemosa *'Plumosa Aurea'. This shrub makes a bright splash of colour and is best used against the darker background of green plants.*

the garden. This will stretch your limited budget by providing you with extra plants to bulk out your existing plantings and also give you a surplus that will enable you to exchange plants with other gardeners. This will then give you the opportunity to provide your garden with a greater variety of suitable plants.

It is essential to start the growth of plants in soil that is completely free of weeds. So important is this need to prepare the ground for the planting of ground cover by the removal of weeds, both annual and perennial, that I have devoted a whole chapter to this subject (*see* Chapter 4). I would encourage the reader to read and heed the advice given. This will save untold troubles in future gardening years.

CHAPTER 3

# Preparing the Soil

For those who are intending to construct new beds or borders or those who already have existing areas which are to be planted with ground cover, the routine of clearing the ground of weeds and all other foreign matter is the same. It is as well here to consider that such areas should be simple in outline, which can be easily kept in good order rather than using complicated layouts which could spell frustration and disappointment at a later date.

The preparation of the soil is, perforce, a long process and can be tedious. However, this early preparatory work is a forerunner to the pleasures that follow with the planting and ultimate accolades you should receive from your neighbours and friends who come to admire the close-knit blend of colour, texture and form of your plant selection.

Whilst the idea of ground cover is to foster a labour-saving garden, it is of little use expecting the plants to thrive if they are planted in grassy or weedy areas. It is essential to give them as good a start as possible in weed-free, well-dug, humus-enriched soil. It must be stressed that the initial cultivation of the area to be planted must be free of all weeds, particularly the deep-rooted perennials and the far-travelling, vigorous ones such as bindweed (*Convolvulus arvensis*), couch grass (*Agropyron repens*) and the creeping buttercup, *Ranunculus repens*.

If the area to be cleared is small and the garden owner feels competent and confident that his

Fig 15  A newly planted front garden. Notice that ample space has been left for plants to develop and so provide good ground cover.

back, his will and his bodily capabilities will stand the strain, then there is no better way to clear the ground than by digging to a one spade depth, breaking up the soil, stooping to gather the weeds, down to the last piece of root and burning all such weed growth. Alternatively, this weed growth can be placed into a strong black plastic bag, together with any unwanted foreign matter that you may come across and the bag then conveyed to the nearest refuse collection point.

For those with larger areas and who feel that such a task is rather too daunting, it is now possible in most areas, to hire a mechanical rotavator of a size that will conveniently fit into the average car. Some hire shops have a delivery and collection service and the machines can usually be hired on a daily basis. However, the picking over and the collecting of the perennial weeds is an integral part of clearing the rotavated ground.

Although the hand digging can be a long drawn out affair, at least one has the satisfaction of knowing that all weed matter has been removed, plus roots and any builders' rubble that there may be. This is particularly relevant if you are starting a new garden or have taken over a neglected one. In the latter, you may find some amazing pieces of not quite antique old iron, tin cans and myriad other signs of human habitation from a long- or not so long-forgotten era. All this rubbish must be consigned to suitable containers or stout sacks and removed from the site. Do not make a pile of this rubbish in your garden until the day comes – which it never does – for its disposal. Otherwise, as the garden progresses, this pile tends to get moved from place to place which is very annoying and time-consuming.

If time allows, cultivate the soil over a period of time to induce germination of annual or perennial weed seeds. The weed seedlings can then be destroyed by hoe or contact weed-killer. This protracted cultivation and leaving of the ground before planting is known as 'fallowing' and ensures that any remnants of perennial weeds can be seen and removed as required.

Modern herbicides, or weed-killers, are tools of recent introduction to the armoury or tool-

Fig 16  *Effective use of the variegated foliage of* Aquilegia.

shed of the modern gardener in the struggle to provide weed-free areas. If the weed-killers are carefully chosen, the planting stage can be reached without the need to leave the ground fallow for an extended period. Chapter 4 deals with weed control and the use of weed-killers (*see* pages 22-25).

## WHAT IS A WEED?

Weeds are plants that are growing where they are not wanted or plants that will interfere with people's use of land for a specific purpose. They so inspire human dislike that attempts are made to eradicate or control them.

The most troublesome weeds are those that spread quickly into soil that has just been cleared.

*Fig 17* Aegopodium podagraria *'Variegatum',
the variegated ground elder. Variegated
'weeds' can be effective to lighten a dark
corner.*

Many spread by seed; some are able to flower
and set seed all year round and can even germinate in the cold of winter. Weeds are not only
vigorous seed producers, they have clever ways
of spreading their seeds.

Bittercress as a weed was not so prevalent
when loam-based composts were the norm. I
am sure that this weed is now to be found in
almost every garden where the owner has introduced plants grown in peat-based composts
and which when bought from even the best-
regulated nurseries and garden centres, will have
potential crops of unwanted bittercress. The ripe
seed pods explode when touched, causing the
seeds to be broadcast far and wide.

The poppy has a stiff stem and a seed pod like
a pepper-pot so that the seeds are shaken into
the new soil by a gust of wind or even by a
'weeding' hand.

Dandelion seeds travel quite a distance,
floating on a little parachute of hairs, as do thistle
seeds. Many weed seeds on waste ground or in
your neighbour's garden can invade your well-
manicured garden by the activities of wind, birds
or animals.

There may be as many as 5,000 seeds in a
square foot (thirty square centimetres) of soil at
any one time. However, they will not all germinate at once. Only a small proportion will do
so in the first year, leaving plenty of seeds to germinate once the soil is cultivated. The soil stores
the seeds until conditions are right for their germination. When seeds are deeply buried, they
remain dormant, but when, with cultivation,
they are brought up near to the surface, the light
and air enables them to grow. It only needs one
or two to grow into plants and to set seed to
start the whole process over again. There are
some weed seeds which germinate as soon as
they are ripe, others wait until the spring,
needing a cold spell to break their dormancy.

Annuals live for one season only but produce
sufficient seeds to reproduce themselves yearly.

Perennials, as their name implies, live for many
years. Their roots can persist in the soil even
though their tops die down in the winter. Some
perennials spread through the ground, sending
up new plants everywhere, and even the tiniest
piece of a root can grow into a new plant. Some
grow so deeply that it is almost impossible to dig
them right out without breaking off a piece of
their brittle root system which, if left in the
ground, will grow into a new and troublesome
plant. Thus it can be seen that different types of
weeds need different treatment to kill them and
eradicate them efficiently.

## Growth Habits of Weeds

Weeds have annual, biennial and perennial
growth habits.

**Annuals** These complete their life cycle in less

*Fig 18   Types of root: (a) spreading root; (b) tap root; (c) deep root; (d) storage root.*

*Fig 19   A colourful border leaving no room for weeds to grow. Height is provided by an Acer in its seasonal colour.*

than one year, growing from seed in the spring and producing seed in the summer or autumn. There is a variation of this life cycle by winter annuals, which germinate in the autumn and live through the winter, completing their seed production in the spring. Annuals thus maintain their population by producing large numbers of seeds. However, only a small percentage will germinate each year. A control programme for annual weeds needs the elimination of young seedlings to prevent seed production.

**Biennials**   These require two seasons to complete their growth and reproductive cycle. A vegetative stage develops during the first season with, usually, the root storing food for over-wintering and then, in the following season, there is new vegetative growth and flowers and seeds are produced. Biennial weeds are best controlled during the vegetative stage during first year of growth.

**Perennials**   These weeds live for two or more years. Such weeds, in addition to producing seed, reproduce and persist by vegetative means, with bulbs, tubers, corms, deep roots, rhizomes or stolons. These multiple reproductive mechanisms make perennial weeds exceedingly difficult to control, for in addition to destroying top growth and preventing seed production, the underground portions must also be eliminated by exacting cultural practices or suitable chemical herbicides. In order to avoid a lot of hard work and discouragement later, one should observe a preventive control measure by stopping all weeds from going to seed and avoiding the use of manures and mulches which are not sterilized.

## Why Do We Weed?

Weeds compete for light, plant food, air and space. They deprive cultivated plants of these essential requirements and so reduce their vigour. Keeping weeds at bay is one of the major occupations of the gardener. Weeds can be unsightly and can quickly swamp cultivated plants that are trying to grow. There are many plants that we might classify as weeds, some are prized and even protected by some groups of the world's population. One man's weed can be another's prized possession in a different environment or country.

## Should We Kill Them All?

Undoubtedly, the vast majority of weeds that appear in our gardens should be dealt with at an early stage, otherwise we will have to accept the consequences. The plants that we grow must not cause inconvenience to other people; if we are to be good neighbours we have to keep strict control over weeds.

However, there is no reason why certain weeds should not be allowed to flourish. Some plants are now rather scarce in the countryside and we, in our gardens, could well encourage a wild area for conservation.

The cowslip, for example, is threatened in the wild in Britain owing to habitat loss and also to over-picking of the flowers which makes it impossible for the plant to set seed for the following year. There are many cultivated plants too that were once, and perhaps still are, weeds growing in their natural habitat. The attractiveness of some species has led to them being grown by specialists and the seeds packaged for enthusiasts to buy and grow in their own gardens.

Modern agricultural practice has reduced the number of flowering weeds in cornfields, such as the bright red common poppy (*Papaver rhoeas*), the yellow corn marigold (*Chrysanthemum segetum*) and the blue cornflower (*Centaurea cyanus*), and these can rarely be seen in the countryside today. Some weeds have attractive seed heads such as the common bistort (*Polygonum bistorta*), teasel (*Dipsacus fullonum*), thrift (*Armeria maritima*) and the wild green hellebore (*Helleborus viridis*). Many of our common grasses of the hedgerows bear graceful heads or 'inflorescences' which look most attractive in a vase with wild flowers.

In recent years, there has been a greater understanding of the need to establish 'conservation areas' in our gardens to protect and encourage a wider range of birds, butterflies, insects and other wildlife. This has been considerably curtailed by man's ever increasing desire to rid himself of the less floriferous and useful plants in favour of those that are highly cultivated with stunning, award winning, colourful blooms. This interest in conservation must be encouraged to maintain our native flora and fauna. Please consider helping this recent movement towards conservation practically if your garden is large enough, by establishing such a haven for our native wildlife.

A nettle patch, for those interested in encouraging butterflies, is an essential requirement. The small tortoiseshell and peacock butterfly caterpillars feed on nettles.

There are many natural remedies and treatments which use some weeds as basic ingredients. The herbal remedies that have been used from ancient times and are still used today are finding favour with many people in this country who prefer to use natural products for the relief of their ailments. The recent trend by many people to put their trust in 'alternative medicine' is indicative of the increasing interest in the environment.

# CHAPTER 4

# Controlling Weeds

## HERBICIDES

Herbicides, or weed-killers, are labour saving and safe when used as directed.

Of the 50 million homes in Great Britain that have a garden, just over sixty per cent of them have householders who profess to being gardeners. Most of them say that they spend too much time controlling weeds, although a very small percentage say that they enjoy weeding.

Statistics show that only forty per cent of gardeners use chemical herbicides in their gardens. Therefore, we might assume that the other twenty per cent weed by hand or hoe and possibly suffer from back pain and muscle damage. Another statistic states that back pain is one of the major causes of absence from work in Britain today. With the judicious use of modern weed-killers, the backache can be taken out of weeding.

The British Association of Herbicide Manufacturers admits that as an industry it has to do a lot of work to convince a greater number of the gardening public that most modern herbicides and garden pesticides, if used according to the maker's instructions, would enable a vast number of people to have a more enjoyable time in their gardens without this drudgery of weeding. Statistics also show that it is the older gardener who is more likely to use weed-killers than the young householder.

## The History of Modern Herbicides

Many of our modern herbicides were developed during research in World War II when the 'miracle' of weed-killers began. Many new chemicals were synthesized and put into use. Prior to this time and early in the century, a very popular weed-killer was sodium arsenate. This was a total weed-killer and was readily available to gardeners despite its poisonous properties.

In post-war years, many compounds and preparations were marketed and some of these are with us to this day. However, some have been totally banned as they have been found to have a cumulative effect in the soil. The disastrous effects of their properties entered the food chain from soil-borne insects through to bird life. Recent Ministry of Agriculture controls in Britain have banned their use because of the unnecessary destruction of wildlife and indeed, in some instances, control was necessary because it was proved that some of these chemicals are harmful to man, for example, the banning of DDT for use as an insecticide.

*Fig 20   Contrasting foliage of bergenias and flowering lavender.*

## Herbicide Control

Herbicides are chemicals that control weed growth. They are pesticides, with the weeds being the pests to be controlled. For the chemicals to be effective as herbicides, they must be toxic against plant material.

A herbicide which is active against most types of plants can be considered a *non-selective* weed-killer. Such chemicals are very useful in areas where complete control of vegetation is desired.

The herbicides for use in lawns are *selective*, that is, the chemical is toxic to certain plants or weeds in the lawn but not to the grass – in other words, the chemical is toxic to some plants and not to others. By using the proper rate of dilution following the maker's instructions on the packet, susceptible weeds can be destroyed in the ground, leaving the more tolerant plants. However, if excessive strengths are used, that is, with a lower dilution, the tolerance may be exceeded, causing injury or death to these tolerant plants – those that you had intended to keep.

Each type of flower, fruit and vegetable varies in its tolerance to a specific herbicide. Therefore, several different herbicides will be required for safe use amongst all the different kinds of plants involved, in order to control different kinds of weeds. Herbicides that are designed to be applied to the soil act on the germinating seeds and young seedlings, therefore, the chemical must persist in the soil during the time when the weed seeds are germinating. Chemicals used for long-term vegetation control will persist in the soil for two or more years, however, some chemical herbicides last for only a few weeks in the soil.

For a chemical to be effective when applied to foliage, it must be retained on the leaf surface so as to penetrate the leaf through its waxy surface barrier and then move inside the plant. Some of the foliar weed-killers have a contact or burning effect on the foliage and do not move inside the plant. Some herbicides are translocated to the growing points – buds, leaves and root tips – and are effective in killing both the above-ground and

*Fig 21* Zantedeschia *'Green Goddess'.*

below-ground parts of the plants. These are ideal and effective against perennial weeds that have vegetative reproductive parts below the soil surface.

Faithfully follow the manufacturer's instructions in the use of weed-killers. Most recommend the use of protective clothing such as gloves. Thoroughly wash out the vessels that have been used and make sure that your hands and face are well washed before eating and drinking. I must repeat, do take note of the instructions given, and be guided by them.

Herbicides may be applied at different times according to the emergence time of the weeds. Most herbicides are designed for mixing with water and can be applied with a watering-can fitted with a rose or drip bar. The use of pressure sprayers in untrained hands is not recommended when total weed-killers are being used. A spray drift can cause harm, disfigurement or death to many treasured plants nearby, either in your own garden or perhaps those of your neighbours.

23

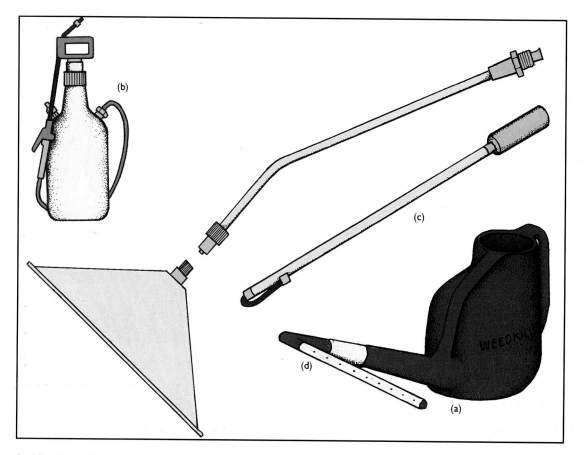

*Fig 22   Weed-killing equipment: (a) a watering-can marked 'weed-killer' and kept exclusively for applying weed-killers or moss-killers to the lawn is a good idea; (b) sprayer; (c) spot weeder; (d) dribble bar.*

For those who do use pressure sprayers, there are now excellent funnel- or cone-shaped ends with special jets that can be fitted to spray lances. These direct the spray to the ground, thus minimizing any chance spray drift (*see* Fig 22). As a precaution, sprayers should only be used on still days without wind to minimize the likelihood of weed-killer blowing on to your wanted plants. Some pre-emergent weed-killers are in the form of granules and pellets and are applied to the soil surface when dry.

Do remember, most herbicides are much more toxic to plants than to people or animals. It is through misuse or careless handling that accidents can occur. Remember the following points:

1.   Do not store weed-killers in unmarked bottles or containers.
2.   Never use milk bottles or lemonade bottles for storage and use at a later date.
3.   Keep your chemicals and herbicides away from children; keep them in a locked cupboard or high up on a shelf in a shed or garage.

The following list should assist you:

**Non-Selective Weed-killers**   Weed-killers con-

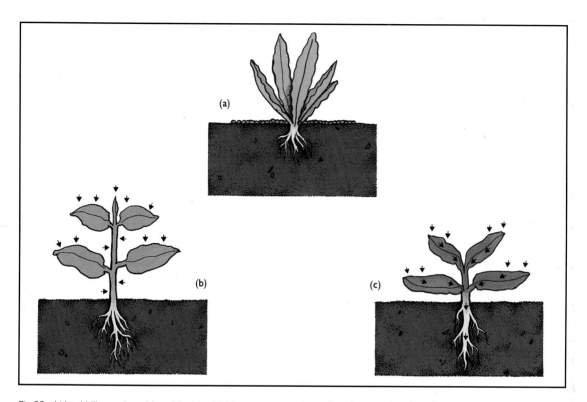

*Fig 23   Weed-killer action. (a) residual herbicides are put on the soil surface so that they do not harm established plant roots but kill the seedlings as they germinate; (b) contact herbicides kill the part of the plant that they touch; (c) translocated herbicides are taken in by the leaves and move down inside the plant to attack the roots.*

taining glyphosate as the active ingredient fell many of our most persistent weeds. It is non-selective and so should never be used in a sprayer for fear that drift might kill other plants including grasses unintentionally.

Ground elder (*Aegopodium podagraria*), horsetail (*Equisetum arvensis*), bindweed (*Convolvulus arvense*) and couch grass (*Agropyron repens*) are killed outright without affecting the soil. With care, a short dribble bar on a watering can will put just enough on the weeds to damp the leaves without run-off. Glyphosate can also be bought as a gel which makes spot treatment easy. The leaves should be painted with the small brush that is inside the container. This weed-killer needs six hours of dry weather immediately after application to get the best results.

### Translocated or leaf acting weed-killers

These herbicides are absorbed by the weed leaves and then move through the plant, eventually killing the roots. They are best used when weeds and grass are in active growth. Such proprietary brands of weed-killers contain amino-triazole and simazine.

**Contact weed-killers**   These kill the parts of the plant that they touch and are not generally carried down to the roots. Proprietary brands contain paraquat and diquat and are de-activated on contact with the soil.

CHAPTER 5

# Improving the Soil

The ideal soil is a neutral loam, but almost invariably in the small suburban garden, such topsoil is often spoiled by builders' rubble and with time, this foreign matter can be dug up and removed.

Heavy clay soils can be lightened and sandy soils enriched. All soils need to have the texture improved by the addition of humus such as compost, farmyard manure, leaf mould, pulverized bark and peat. However, with the current concern about the way in which we are depleting our peat deposits in Britain, there is a quest to find alternative composts. Some success has been achieved with the use of coconut fibre mixed with a sterilized by-product recycled from household waste. Spent hops are an ideal compost if you live near a brewery.

On the other hand, if you live somewhere near a mushroom farm, then spent mushroom compost, which is animal manure mixed with peat,

is excellent for digging into the soil when well rotted. However, the mushroom grower does add quite a high percentage of lime to this compost and this in turn will, if used regularly, raise the content of lime in your soil and therefore raise the pH. For those who would like to grow ericaceous plants and who have a neutral to acid soil in the garden, then spent mushroom compost is not for you.

We can, as has been said, choose plants that are most suitable for the soil in our gardens, and no better ground cover can be found for those with acid soils than the Ericas, the Heaths and the Heathers.

Whatever your soil and microclimate, set out to make the best of your situation with the plants that are available; don't try to fight nature.

## MULCHES

### Enriching the Soil and Foliar Feeding

A layer of 3in (7cm) or more of thick mulching material placed between ground cover plants is an excellent method of suppressing weed growth. This also encourages the rapid development of the plants by conserving moisture. Make sure that the mulch, if home-made, is not contaminated with weed seeds.

Peat, pulverized bark, well-rotted farmyard manure, leaf mould and mushroom compost are excellent mulches. Even with a good, thick, heavy mulch, it is inevitable that some weed seeds will be blown on to the mulch and will germinate. However, the growth of such weed seeds will be

Fig 24 Aegopodium podograria 'Variegatum', the variegated ground elder, is good ground cover if it has a restricted root run.

*Fig 25  Massed planting of flowering bulbs used to good effect as seasonal ground cover.*

lush so that they can be easily seen and removed. Do ensure that the mulch goes between the plants and not on top of them.

Regular mulching in the spring, between the clump-forming plants until they grow together, will not only help weed control but will improve the humus content of the soil. Once your ground cover plants have spread into one another, it is difficult to get the mulch in between the plants and on to the soil. This can be managed by sprinkling a little at a time between the stems to help to keep the humus supplied to the soil. Please be warned, do not put mulch over the top of carpeting or colonizing plants as it could smother them. A little at a time and often, is the solution. There are many alternatives to peat that make good mulching materials (*see* Chapter 8).

## FERTILIZERS

If your ground is in poor heart, you can resort to adding artificial fertilizers mixed in with the mulch, or an organic fertilizer such as bone-meal or hoof and horn.

Around 1973, a slow-release fertilizer was evolved consisting of capsules of ordinary concentrated fertilizer, wrapped in a coat of natural resin extracted from soya beans. Each capsule is

about the size of a wheat grain. By a process similar to osmosis, dissolved nutrients move slowly out through the resinous coating into the surrounding soil to be taken up by the fine root hairs of the plants.

These fertilizers are prepared in a number of ways so that not only is the speed controlled at which the capsules release their contents, but also the ingredients are varied to meet the requirements of particular plants. The thicker the capsule coating, the slower the release of the fertilizer.

These are the small round brown or pale blue capsules that are seen in pots of plants obtained from a nursery or garden centre. These capsules have been the subject of much correspondence to editors of gardening magazines and the technical enquiry desk at horticultural shows such as the Royal Horticultural Society's shows in London. Gardeners, when finding these capsules in pots and not knowing what they are, presume them to be the eggs of some garden pest. However, in the context of fertilizer for the garden, they are much too expensive to be used and were really designed for pot-grown plants.

Care should be taken to ensure that artificial fertilizers are watered in after broadcasting them over the soil – this prevents foliar scorching. Foliar feeds can be recommended. An application of diluted liquid feed sprayed on to the leaves will result in the nutrients being quickly absorbed. Foliar feeding can produce a rapid response from the plants if applied at the right time. The most effective times are late spring and early summer. Foliar feeds on a silver or grey border where the plants have hairy leaves is not necessary or desirable as their use will result in over-vigorous, 'leggy' plants. The main value of foliar feeding is to invigorate and feed plants that are backward in growth, perhaps those with a poor root system or those that are not yet established.

*Fig 26 (opposite)   The colourful leaves of Hedera helix 'Buttercup' making an excellent mat of ground cover. Many ivies, used in this way, are effective, in suppressing weeds.*

*Fig 27   Good ground-hugging planting, contrasting with the gravel and brick pathway.*

I stress that the top layer of fertile soil, with the addition of humus, and long-lasting organic fertilizers, will give your plants the impetus that they need. If this extra care is given, you will be well rewarded for your efforts with healthy, well-nourished plants.

## THE COMPOST HEAP

Annual weeds can be added to the compost heap, the growth should be soft and without seed heads. As a general rule, and for the beginner in compost heap making, I suggest that you do not put in perennial weeds such as the deep-rooted dandelion (*Taraxacum officinale*), thistle (*Cirsium* sp.) and bindweed (*Convolvulus arvensis*). It is essential that any seed viability within the rotting material be destroyed by the heating process, which occurs naturally in a compost heap, and by fermentation.

# CHAPTER 6

# Plants for Ground Cover

## HEATHERS

As evergreens, heathers contribute interest to the garden throughout the year but their use is restricted to soils which are neutral to acid. However, there are a few species that will tolerate alkaline soils. When planted in groups, each grows into its neighbour, making superb ground cover and leaving little opportunity for weeds to grow.

Heathers can be effective when planted in small groups along the foot of shrub borders or beds. They have been used for formal edging along the sides of paths and there have been most effective beds consisting entirely of heathers grown with dwarf or slow-growing conifers and other suitable shrubs. It is usual to plant a collection of ground cover heaths and heathers in bold groups to form a patchwork which, with careful choice of varieties, will provide all year round colour from flowers and foliage. Heathers can thrive in a wide range of conditions but certainly need to be in sunshine, otherwise they tend to become leggy and straggly, soft in growth and fail to flower.

Heaths and heathers (*Erica*, *Daboecia* and *Calluna*) have deservedly gained recognition for their wide and effective use in the modern garden. Their various sizes, habit of growth, colour of flower and foliage, their flowering times and the way in which they blend with other plants in the garden, such as small trees and shrubs, can result in one of the most satisfying of garden features.

There are many species of *Erica* growing wild in southern Africa where they have the common name of cape heathers, but these are not hardy in Britain. The heathers of moorland and mountain in Britain and Europe are the hardy heathers.

**Ericas and Callunas** *Ericas* are evergreen plants with small, linear leaves. The hardy species are native to Europe and eight or nine of the species readily can be found growing wild in Britain. Their flowers are produced in abundance on the end of the growing shoots. These flowers do not drop when they die but remain on the stems, turning to an attractive red-brown colour.

*Erica* is the botanical name for the heaths and *Calluna* the name for heathers. However, we have come to include both *Calluna* and *Erica* in the term heather – as in the heather garden. *Calluna vulgaris* is a purple heather. However, over many years plant growers have selected considerable variations in the habit of growth and the colour of flower and foliage.

*Erica carnea* has been known by that name for many, many years in nursery catalogues. However, it is possible that it may be labelled as *E. herbacea*, its more recent name, in some nurseries and garden centres. *Erica* has the invaluable quality of growing and making a self-maintaining area of garden. The evergreen foliage makes a deep and almost impenetrable carpet over the ground. The carpet will stay dense without the clipping that other heathers need in order to achieve the same effect. This plant is extremely useful for growing on sloping grass banks where there are outcrops of rock, and in association with some well-chosen shrubs. This can

Fig 28 Colourful heathers as ground cover, contrasting with conifers, growing in Bressingham, Norfolk.

transform a troublesome area into one of low maintenance.

*Erica carnea* and its many cultivars will tolerate alkaline soils. In Britain they can be seen growing successfully on a north-facing bank at the Royal Horticultural Society's garden at Wisley in Surrey and at Windsor Great Park. For those of you who garden in the Norfolk area, a visit to Mr Adrian Bloom's garden at Diss on one of his many open days, will show you superb examples of this type of planting.

**Daboecias** *Daboecia cantabrica* is a native of Ireland. It grows rather tall to about 2ft (60cm). The broad leaves are dark green above and whitish below. The oval flowers are a rosy purple and are borne at the ends of the shoots from early June until late summer. There are several white-flowered forms of *Daboecia cantabrica* that have a similar growth habit but with paler foliage and somewhat larger flowers. Generally, native British 'heathers' enjoy, in the broad sense, much the same growing conditions. In the wild, they tend to grow in harsh environments with poor soil and little shelter. With a little care given to them in the garden, they will earn their keep for many seasons, providing that it is remembered that heathers must be planted in full sun.

## Soil Preparation

I must emphasize that it is necessary to prepare the soil thoroughly before planting to achieve vigorous and healthy growth of the chosen plants.

Dig over the area for planting well and remove all weeds. In particular, remove all perennial weeds such as bindweed and couch grass. These weeds are otherwise very difficult to control after the area has been planted. Chapter 3, Preparing the Soil, should be referred to (see p. 16).

Work in quantities of ericaceous peat ensuring that the peat is damp. This is an acidic peat. In heavy clay soils, drainage can be improved by mixing in sharp grit and raising the level of the bed to a few inches above the surrounding soil. Extra peat will also help to improve the texture of a heavy soil.

In lighter, sandy soils, heathers can be grown satisfactorily, though in hot, dry weather, the drainage will be rather too rapid. The water-holding capacity of this type of soil can be improved by the ample mixing in of peat or compost. In the spring, extra peat or compost should be mixed in around the plants.

## Mulching

An annual mulch with peat in spring is beneficial, after the heather has been pruned. The peat should be worked between the plants to form a layer of about 1in (2cm) deep. Pulverized bark and peat is an alternative mulching material. This mulch will help to conserve moisture in the soil and will also act as a weed supressant.

## Planting Heathers

Heathers look their best in informal beds in the sunniest part of the garden. They can also be planted to great effect in large tubs and troughs, both in the larger rock gardens and in the front of herbaceous or shrub borders. Heathers are excellent for sites in the garden where extra colour and ground cover are needed. The winter-flowering heathers can be grown in the larger hanging baskets, window-boxes and planters where they will brighten the dullest months of the year.

Water all plants thoroughly before removing from the black polythene bag or pot, trying not to disturb the root ball. Using a hand trowel, make a hole, which should be the same size as the root ball, in the prepared soil. Sprinkle in a large pinch of bone-meal and insert the root ball,

firming the soil around it. Finally, work a mixture of moist peat and bone-meal into the crown of the plant.

## Planting Density Guide for Maximum Effect

For winter- and spring-flowering heathers such as the hybrid *Erica × darleyensis*, the planting density is three plants per square yard (1 square metre). *Erica carnea* (or *E. herbacea*) which also flowers in winter and spring, needs five plants per square yard (1 square metre). Both these types are suitable for alkaline soils that have a degree of chalk in their content.

For summer- and autumn-flowering varieties of *Calluna vulgaris*, use a density of five plants per square yard (1 square metre). These are, perhaps, the most popular as they have many varieties with coloured foliage which is also good for winter effect.

These guides to planting should produce, in two to three years, a superb carpet of colourful, evergreen ground cover.

## Caring for Heathers

Particular care is needed during the year of planting. Water the plants thoroughly when they are planted and maintain a watering programme to prevent the plants from drying out. Hand weed until the plants grow together and cover the ground.

### Pruning

It is essential to prune heathers to keep the plants in shape and to encourage new growth and flowers. Use sharp shears to trim off shoots that have flowered, being careful not to cut into old wood. Shape the plants into neat mounds and cut back excessive lateral growths to prevent them from encroaching upon other plants.

Prune summer-flowering heathers immediately after the flowers have faded. Winter-flowering heathers should be pruned in late spring. Autumn-flowering heathers should have their withered flowers removed in spring and late spring-flowering varieties can have their flowering growths removed as soon as they have faded and withered.

## How to Buy Heathers

Although there are relatively few species of heather, there are hundreds of cultivars, varying in flower colour, time of flowering and leaf colour.

All good nurseries and garden centres have seasonal displays of heathers. One-year-old plants in 3in (7–9cm) pots are a good buy, although larger plants offered by some establishments will give a more instant effect. Select strong, bushy plants, read the labels and check ultimate height of growth and the flowering season. Buy those plants that will suit the particular requirements of your garden; whether you choose summer- or winter-flowering heathers depends very much on your type of soil.

Planting several plants of one variety together will create a bold splash of colour. Some heathers are naturally upright in growth – others are more compact and some have a spreading habit.

There are many new *Calluna vulgaris* varieties available and among those to be recommended are:-

**C.v. 'Annemarie'**   A plant with long spikes of double, rosy-red flowers.

**C.v. 'Cottswood Gold'**   A good yellow foliaged form that does not scorch as much as some yellows.

**C.v. 'Hillbrook Orange'** and **C.v. 'Red Carpet'** Both have very good red foliage, excellent for planting on exposed sites.

**Erica manipuliflora** varieties are happy in alkaline soils. They have beautiful scented flowers but can be rather tall growing rather than ground covering in habit.

**Erica carnea (E. herbacea)**   This may be found under either name in the nursery or garden centre.

**E.c. 'Challenger', 'Myretoun Ruby'** and **'Walter Reisert'**   These are good winter flowering heaths. 'Golden Starlet' is an unusual yellow foliaged variety with white flowers, other yellow leaved clones have pink flowers.

**E.x. darleyensis 'Kramer's Roter'**   This is very colourful with rich ruby flowers on bronze-green foliage and contrasts well with *E.x. darleyensis* 'White Perfection'.

Autumn flowering heathers, as a general rule, do not like lime in the soil. However, *Erica vagans* will tolerate an alkaline situation. Flowering in August, it can be obtained with red, pink or white flowers. When clipped over in spring, it keeps a lively green moss-like colouring in winter. Winter flowering varieties will also tolerate a hint of lime in the soil, they have white or pink flowers and a good range of reds. Also flowering in winter and early spring are hybrids with similar white, pink and red flower colourings.

Among the best are *E.x. darleyensis* 'Molten Silver' also known as 'Silberschmelze' or 'Silver Bells' which is white flowered, 'Arthur Johnson' (syn. A.T. Johnson') a good mauve and the pink flowered 'Darley Dale'.

Those who garden on acid soil will be able to plant *Erica cinerea* which, in its many coloured flowering forms, offers the brightest colouring of the entire family. Acid soils also make it possible to grow the autumn flowering varieties of *Calluna* which have perhaps the greater variety of flower colour, including some that have gold and silver in the leaves.

## Propagating Your Own Heather Plants

### Seeds

Some heather plants can be raised from seed

and self-sown seedlings can often be seen growing near the parent plant.

Other methods of increasing plant stock are by rooting cuttings or by layering.

## Cuttings

Probably the most successful way to increase plant stock is by taking cuttings which will produce sufficient roots in three to six weeks, depending upon the species or cultivar. Heathers of almost any variety provide ample cutting material. Cuttings can be taken at almost any time from April to July, provided that the parent plant is healthy and growing well. Look for shoots that are 2in (5–6cm) long, pulling them from the parent plant and taking with them a small portion of the firmer wood – a heel cutting.

Trim the heel cuttings with a sharp knife and dip them into hormone rooting powder. Between twenty and thirty cuttings can be inserted into a 5in (13cm) pan, setting them about 1in (2cm) deep in a mixture of half peat and half horticultural grit. Do not use builders' sand. Give the cuttings and compost a good soaking, using a fine rose on a watering can, and leave them in a shady place or cold frame. The cuttings should root in a month or so.

Once rooted, pot them up individually into 2½in (6cm) pots, using a compost of two parts acid loam, two parts moss peat and one part sharp sand. Alternatively, use any proprietary ericaceous potting compost of which there are many brands on the market. Keep the plants shaded and suitably watered.

For those of you with a cold frame, these young, recently potted plants should be hardened off by placing them within the closed frame and gradually, over a period, opening the frame to allow more air to circulate. These should make excellent bushy plants to set out into the garden the following summer or autumn.

## Layering

A few branches around the edge of the plant can be selected and pegged into the ground so that a few inches of the stems are buried. Loosen the surface of the soil and mix in a little horticultural grit and peat and fix the selected stems into this by using wooden pegs or bent wires.

This method is very successful if carried out in late September or October. It will take about a year for sufficient roots to be established when it is then possible to cut the new plants from the parent.

Ideally, these new plants should be put into a shady part of the garden where they can grow on for about six months before they are planted into permanent positions.

## Problems with Heathers

Fortunately, heaths and heathers in gardens are seldom affected by pests. Heather beetle and midge gall blight are more usually found in heathers growing on moorlands.

Erica wilt or browning has become troublesome in certain cultivars. This can be noticed by the silvering of leaves on one or two shoots, the tips of which wilt, resulting in the ultimate die-back of the shoots which turn brown.

There is little control for this problem for the amateur and home gardener and it is best to dig up such plants and burn them.

## CONIFERS

Conifers are ideal plants to form the basis of an all-year-round garden. Their textured evergreen foliage provides a permanent backdrop and foil for other plants.

Conifers also make excellent hedges and windbreaks, particularly so when the golden hybrid × Cupressocyparis 'Castlewellan Gold' is used, which is so attractive in the winter.

Other choices for hedging could be forms of Thuja occidentalis, Thuja plicata, Chamaecyparis nootkatensis and the well-known C. lawsoniana. There is an upright form of Thuja which makes a thick wall of a good dark green at all times of the year. This is *Thuja occidentalis* 'Holmstrup' which is usually a rich green but can appear to have a purple-brown colouring, particularly in winter. *T. plicata*, with its polished leaves, has a quite noticeable, very pleasant resinous smell and looks very good when well clipped. *T.p.* 'Zebrina' is the striped form and whilst being basically green, there are bands of pale cream and gold on the young growth, giving a quite yellow appearance.

Planting a horizontal growing conifer next to one of narrowly erect habit is effective. The contrast of growing habit enhances the character of each. The fastigiate or narrow columnar varieties are useful small trees for small spaces and lend proportion to the garden design. There are, however, many excellent prostrate forms of conifers that will clothe awkward corners or banks and they can help to cover the surface of bare retaining walls.

Used as ground cover, conifers smother weeds very efficiently and junipers lead the field in their ground covering ability. They are valuable aesthetically and practically and their neat, level, horizontal growth makes them suitable for formal and informal planting. Some gardeners have used them successfully as edgings to flower borders, provided a dark foil and change of texture to the riot of flower colour. Conifers are available in a variety of tints of green with some having leaves of a quite golden colour.

## Pruning

Generally, conifers require very little pruning other than the tidying up of stray growth to keep the plants shapely. If you want a compact plant or a special shape, then little and often is the safe pruning rule.

Some of the horizontal growing conifers benefit from being trained to keep to the horizontal and such plants should have this training early in life. If necessary, the branches should be pegged down to encourage their natural growing habit.

Fig 29   A conifer softening the well-kept lawn edges.

## Planting and Ultimate Growth Size

Pot- and container-grown conifers can be planted all the year round provided that ample water is given during dry periods. They do not require rich soil or manure, but sandy or clay soils will need to be improved by mixing in a proportion of peat or leaf-mould. Plant 1in (2cm) deeper than the level of the soil in the container and firm the surrounding soil well down against the root ball, having teased out the roots in the lower part of the root ball in order to spread them out in the hole that has already been made. The size to which a conifer will grow depends very much on the soil, position and climate. There is no ultimate size as such, for a conifer will keep on

*Fig 30   A border of mixed heathers and conifers growing in Bressingham, Norfolk.*

growing throughout its life. For guidance, I have given expected growth sizes after a ten year period in average soils.

## The Horizontal or Prostrate Growing Forms

**Junipers** *Juniperus* is a very large genus with more than forty species. mainly evergreen, extremely hardy and tough, they can tolerate hot, dry conditions well and can be safely planted in limy soils. However, they are prone to damage by aphids and scale insects. These pests should be controlled by a regular spraying with a good proprietary systemic insecticide.

*Juniperus communis depressa* 'Gold Clone' is a slow growing, spreading plant with clear yellow new shoots turning to old gold. It has a spread of between 2–3 feet (0.60–0.9lm), and grows to a height of 9in(23cm).

*J.c.* 'Hornibrookii' has a prostrate growth habit, spreading to a width of between 3–4 feet (0.9lm–1.22m), and has grey-green foliage.

*J.c.* 'Minima' is sometimes listed as 'Silver Lining'. The foliage is glaucous green with a silver sheen. It has a prostrate growth habit, forming a plant of 3 feet (0.9lm) in width.

*J. horizontalis* 'Plumosa Compacta' forms a flat-topped, wide spreading plant reaching a width of 2 feet 6 inches (0.76m). The leaves are a light green which become plum purple in winter.

*J.h.* 'Wiltonii', sometimes listed as 'Glauca' and *J.h.* 'Blue Chip' are two forms with brilliant steel-blue leaves. Both form a dense mat with an approximate growth spread of 4 feet (1.22m).

*J. × media* 'Old Gold' and *J. × media* 'Mint Julep'. The former has leaves of a rich gold and the latter has mint green foliage. Both have a dense spreading growth habit reaching to between 3 and 4 feet (0.9lm–1.22m).

*J. virginiana* 'Silver Spreader' is a low growing plant with silver-grey foliage, reaching 2–3 feet (0.60–0.9lm) across. There is a form of *J. virginiana*, 'Grey Owl' that has grey-green leaves with yellow stems. This has a similar growth rate to the above.

**Yew** *Taxus* is a genus of six or seven species. All are very hardy and accommodating with regard to soil and situation. Their leaves are generally a dark, rich green, sometimes almost a black-green. When planting the low and spreading forms, it is wise to mix these in with other cultivars that have striking golden and variegated forms.

36

*Taxus baccata* 'Adpressa', which I understand has appeared in the wild from time to time, forms a large spreading shrub with densely crowded branches and small, dark green leaves.

*T.b.* 'Adpressa Aurea' has a similar growth habit, somewhat less vigorous, with golden yellow foliage and a growth rate of about 1–2in (2–5cm) per year.

*T.b.* 'Dwarf White' is a slow-growing low bush with a spread of 2–3 feet (0.60–0.9lm). The leaves are variegated with a silver margin.

*T.b.* 'Repens Aurea' is a prostrate plant with bright yellow variegation, achieving a spread of between 2 feet 6 inches and 3 feet (0.76 and 0.9lm).

*T.b.* 'Pumila Aurea' has a somewhat irregular growth habit which is slightly upright, with spreading branches and foliage of a rich golden yellow. Growth rate is approximately 2in (5cm) per year.

## Recommended Fastigiate Forms for Accent

*Taxus baccata* 'Fastigiata' has good dark green foliage and bears red berries in early autumn. It will grow to 6–8 feet (1.8–2.4m) in height with a spread of approximately 15in (38cm).

*T.b.* 'Fastigiata Aurea' is a little slower in growth, reaching a height of 6 feet (1.8m) with a 15in (38cm) spread. The foliage is golden yellow, turning to green in the second year. The red berries appear in early autumn.

*T.b.* 'Standishii' has a very narrow growth habit, reaching a height of only just over 2 feet (0.60m) with a spread of 8in (20cm). It has rich golden foliage, producing red berries late in the year.

## Horizontal Forms

*Picea pungens* 'Glauca Prostrata' has a stiffly

*Fig 31   Juniper and golden* Viburnum opulus *'Aureum Compactum'.*

horizontal growth habit with aromatic silver blue foliage, reaching to between 12–15 inches (30–36cm) in height and 5 feet (1.50m) in width.

Tsuga canadensis 'Cole' has green foliage, and the long branches grow to 3–4 feet (0.90–1.20m) following the contours of soil or rock and forming an extensive carpet 3–6inches (8–15cm) in height.

## FERNS

Although many hardy ferns are not totally evergreen, there are a few that retain their leaves sufficiently well to be attractive during the winter months. They are ideal plants to be grown in the shadier parts of the garden or in shady beds at the side of the house where little else will grow, providing that one remembers to keep the soil moist by watering occasionally. These areas are often excessively dry as they are under the eaves of the house and are likely to receive little or no natural rainfall.

Ferns are excellent for planting in shaded beds on terraces, or in courtyards such as those that abound in our modern suburban blocks of flats. Areas like these are often in subdued light throughout the day because of the towering walls of the buildings. So often in these develop-

Fig 32   A cool area devoted to ferns.

*Fig 33  A typical English spring scene of* Narcissus, buttercups, bluebells and ferns.

ments, such areas are planted seasonally with flowers that soon fade and become untidy.

There are varieties of ferns that do well in town gardens and do not object to the occasional gentle hosing to remove dirt and dust. They can be used to provide verdant underplanting for trees and shrubs and the only maintenance needed is the yearly trim of any withered fronds.

The popularity of ferns has waned from their heyday in Victorian times, and without the demand, nurserymen have naturally allowed their stocks to diminish. However, there are many rare species that have survived in Britain through the efforts of devoted admirers of ferns, particularly the members of the British Pteridological Society. Ferns are now enjoying a revival and we can at least obtain our plants today from specialist nurseries. Some of the more popular ferns are now finding their way into stocks at the larger garden centres whose knowledgeable buyers are forever looking out for new and interesting lines.

Many types of fern grow naturally in open woodland, some by woodland streams, whilst others are found at the bottom of hedges or in deep crevices between outcrops of limestone. It is thus evident that the provision of some shade with a cool root run and protection from strong winds are the factors which will provide the best results. Whilst there are some ferns that love to grow in moist conditions, very few will thrive in badly drained, heavy clay soils, in full sun or in windy and draughty positions.

There is an exquisite delicacy in their unfolding fronds in spring and early summer. I can assure you that you will not be disappointed in my recommendation to include them in your garden.

Once established in good soil with some humus, they will increase yearly and will thrive in limy soils as well as in acid soil. Some ferns can even delight us with their autumn colours. Above all, a well-grown area of ferns provides a dainty filigree of leaves which suppress annual weeds and thereby constitute excellent ground cover.

As with all the plants dealt with in this book, it is essential to ensure that the ground is clean and free from all perennial weeds before planting up the chosen area.

The male fern, *Dryopteris filix-mas* will thrive at the foot of shrubs or a privet hedge, and even in the poorest, possibly rubble filled, area of soil that is in a more sunny position. If you have really moist ground, the royal fern, *Osmunda regalis* is the most handsome of hardy ferns. It can achieve a height of 6 feet (2 metres) in ideal soils and its attractive fronds turn to yellow and a bright brown in autumn. It is not a 'traveller' but a solid clump former, whereas the handsome, dark green fern, *Blechnum chilense* will spread, as will the fresh green, deciduous sensitive fern, *Onoclea sensibilis*.

Most ferns, however, are clump formers in the normal soil in our gardens, and there is no better than the delicate lady fern, *Athyrium filix-femina*, of which there are many forms with strange, crested and bifurcated leaves.

There are shorter-growing ferns, such as the drought-resistant common polypody, *Polypodium vulgare* which, incidentally, is evergreen and can make a most attractive spreading carpet. In this species, there are many clones with attractive variants in the leaf outlines.

## Where to Plant Ferns

The north side of a house or other building, or a boundary wall which prevents exposure to direct sunlight, are suitable places to plant ferns. This type of shade is better than that provided by overhanging branches of trees, as the drips from the trees are detrimental to some ferns. If the trees are not directly overhead, ferns will be quite happy in the dappled shade cast by the branches. Trouble can arise from overhead foliage if the trees become infested with greenfly. This causes the dropping of honeydew on to the fern fronds. This sticky secretion encourages the growth of black mould which discolours the fern fronds and impairs their ability to manufacture foods.

Having selected the most suitable position for planting, the ground should be well prepared by digging over to about 12in (30cm) depth, breaking up the soil and mixing in liberal dressings of leaf-mould and moist, fibrous peat. If the soil is at all heavy, especially if it is a very dense clay, quantities of coarse grit should be added to improve the drainage.

The vast majority of ferns do not present any particular difficulty in cultivation. Many will survive the most indifferent treatment as they can be seen surviving in old gardens that have endured years of neglect. However, it is wise to provide the most favourable conditions for good root action and healthy development of the foliage.

## Growing Ferns with Other Plants

There are quite a few plants that appreciate cool conditions and some shade which will associate and contrast well with ferns, particularly those with bolder foliage.

The hardy bear's breeches, *Acanthus mollis* has deeply lobed foliage and makes a large, bushy plant, and *Acanthus spinosus* is particularly decorative with rather spiny foliage. For the front of the fern border, try Bergenias which are usually evergreen and whose leaves adopt a reddish autumn colouring.

Fig 34   A shaded and effective woodland setting with a meandering path through shade –
and moisture-loving plants.

As an alternative to this planting suggestion, there are numerous spring bulbs and corms, including snowdrops, that if planted in front of the ferns, can make a most effective display. *Convallaria majalis*, lily of the valley, is a useful ground cover plant. It can be invasive, but the beauty and sweetness of the flowers more than compensate for the need to keep the plants within bounds. There is a superb variegated leaf form and also one which has rather small, pale, pink flowers.

A curiosity is *Arisarum proboscideum*, the mouse plant. This makes mats of polished green,

arrow-shaped leaves that are carried a few inches off the ground. The flowers are the oddity since they resemble mice slipping into hiding, waving their tails behind them.

*Dicentra spectabilis*, bleeding heart, is also suitable for the shady border with its attractive fern-like foliage. There are other smaller, *Dicentras* that grow well in semi-shade and are useful for foreground use and these may be obtained with flowers that are pink or white.

*Epimedium*, barrenworts, like shady conditions and the flowers can be white, pink, yellow or orange. They all have green, heart-shaped

41

*Fig 35 Good ground cover can be provided with a clump of* Acanthus spinosus.

leaves which turn to gorgeous leaf colourings in the autumn.

Many of the hellebores will associate well with ferns but would be best used in a wide border to accommodate several clumps of plants.

The contrasting foliage of hostas, particularly those with striking variegated leaves, make a good showing when interplanted with ferns.

There are various species of *Polygonatum*, Solomon's seal, that can give a good account of themselves when planted with ferns. Their usually quite glaucous foliage on tall stems carry flowers of dangling white bells.

*Anemone nemorosa*, the native European woodland wildflower, has many colour forms, as has the Mediterranean *Anemone blanda*. Both flower in the spring and both will grow well in the front of the bed where ferns have been planted.

## Indigenous and Non-Indigenous Ferns Hardy in Britain

Ferns were extremely popular in the late nineteenth century with many of the larger households having specially constructed, glazed fern houses which seldom included ferns from foreign parts. Although at this time plant hunters were sending home many exotic and worthwhile flowering plants for our gardens and stovehouses, scant attention seems to have been paid to the possibilities of ferns that might be hardy in Britain.

Estimates vary, but there are between 10,000 and 12,000 known fern species world-wide, the majority occurring in the tropics and sub-tropics. Many of these species have most interesting and diverse forms and the list below, with brief descriptions will, I hope, encourage you to seek them out in nurseries and garden centres to plant in your gardens. Of course, it goes without saying that these plants should on no account be dug up from their wild habitats.

## Hardy Ferns Indigenous to Britain

**Asplenium scolopendrium** (hart's tongue fern) An easy to grow evergreen fern with fronds that have a smooth, leathery, strap-like appearance. Will grow to a height of 18–24in (46–60cm).

**A.s. 'Crispum'** (crisped hart's tongue fern) The margins of the fronds are beautifully crimped, giving a frilled appearance.

**A.s. 'Crispum' nobile** This has a wider, deeply ruffled leaf and is taller growing.

**A.s. 'Cristatum'** (crested hart's tongue fern) The frond divides about a third of the way along, then re-divides to end in large crests of tassels.

**A.s. digitatum** A cristate form with branching flat crests separated like the fingers of a hand.

**A.s. laceratum** The fronds are shorter growing, measuring about 4in (10cm) wide with deeply cut margins, the tips sometimes crested.

**Asplenium trichomanes** (maidenhair spleenwort) Ideal for crevices or shady walls, this is good little fern excellent for growing with dwarf bulbs.

**A.t. cristata** A crested form of the above.

**Athyrium filix-femina** (lady fern) The finely divided fronds can grow up to 4 feet (1.3metres) in length according to conditions and variety. The green fronds have a fine, lacy appearance.

**A. filix-femina cristatum** Flat, fan-like crests form on the apex of the fronds and the plant will grow to about 2–3 feet (0.6–1m).

**A. filix-femina 'Fieldii'** The long, narrow fronds grow up to 3 feet (1 metre) in length and the short pinnae are angled and set in pairs which cross over each other.

**A. filix-femina 'Frizelliae'** (tatting fern) The fronds are very narrow with the pinnae contracted into flattish balls which look like a necklace of green beads.

**A. filix-femina 'Victoriae'** The very slender, tasselled fronds have paired pinnules that cross over one another.

**Dryopteris** (buckler ferns) These are all robust plants providing large, handsome clusters of verdant growth and are more or less problem free in cultivation.

**Dryopteris dilatata 'Grandiceps'** Dense, ball-shaped crests at the ends of the fronds make this a most attractive plant.

**D. filix-mas** (male fern) A very good plant for the woodland or wild garden which can reach up to 5 feet (1.75 metres). The feathery, lance-shaped fronds are a lightish-green.

**D. filix-mas 'Crispa'** A good dwarf form with compact fronds, this will grow to about 12–18in (30–46cm).

**D. filix-mas 'Crispa Cristata'** This is a fairly dwarf form with the fronds well crisped and neatly crested.

**D. filix-mas 'Depauperata'** The glossy, dark green fronds have narrow pinnae and reduced segments.

**D. pseudo-mas** The golden green fronds become darker as they mature and the plant can grow to 2–5 feet (0.60–1.75 metres).

**D. pseudo-mas cristata 'The King'** A really magnificent fern with a bold and striking habit which will grow to about 2–3 feet (0.60–1 metre).

**Gymnocarpium dryopteris 'Plumosum'** (oak fern) The triple headed fronds open out to delicately traced triangles of vivid green on a single slender stem. This fern could be planted in stony soil in a shady part of the rock garden or at the front of a fern border.

**Osmunda regalis** (Royal fern) This fern should be grown in acid soil and makes a magnificent specimen growing to 3–6 feet (1–2 metres). It likes plenty of moisture and the fronds are a deep green with a leathery texture.

**O.r. cristata** This is a crested form of the above.

**Polypodium vulgare** (common polypody) A useful evergreen with smooth, leathery, elongated and lance-shaped fronds which are deeply cut. It prefers to be planted in stony ground and the growth can vary from 3–18in (7–46cm).

**P.v. 'Bifido cristatum'** This variety has long narrow fronds terminating in a wide crest.

**P.v. interjectum** The fronds are ovate to lanceolate with the basal pinnae bending inwards. The growth size is about 9–15in (23–38cm).

**Polystichum aculeatum** (hard shield fern) This fern will do well in almost any position but is particularly good for woodland planting. The leathery fronds are glossy on top and matt beneath.

**P. setiferum** (soft shield fern) An elegant fern with graceful arching fronds of a softer texture than those of the above. It is easy to grow and will produce large clumps when given moisture and shade.

**P.s. congestum** A good dwarf form with dense, upright fronds.

**P.s. divisilobum** In early spring, the unfolding

fronds are deeply clothed with white scales which look most attractive. The mature fronds are large and will grow flat along the ground with the tips pointing upwards.

**P.s. 'Plumosum'** The fronds are very finely divided with very overlapping pinnae. Growth size is about 18–30in (46–76cm).

## Hardy Ferns Non-Indigenous to Britain

**Adiantum pedatum** (N. American maidenhair fern) A beautiful fern with slender purplish black stems bearing many-fingered flat, fan-like blades. This plant likes a good rich humus soil.

**A.p. aleuticum** A dwarf variety very suitable for the rock garden. It grows in mounds of dense and delicate pale green, glaucous fronds.

**A.p. venustum** The triangular ovate fronds are soft green in spring but have a bluish tinge when mature.

**Athyrium niponicum pictum** The broadly triangular fronds have pointed tips and the grey-green pinnae merge to green at the margin. This should be planted in a sheltered position.

**Blechnum penna marina** (dwarf hard fern) A tiny creeping species with small, leathery fronds that lie flat which are usually about 6in (15cm) long at the maximum. It will spread easily as it has a vigorous creeping rootstock.

**Dryopteris atrata** A graceful fern with deep green, lance-shaped, arching fronds and can grow to 2–3ft (0.60–1m).

**D. erythrosora** (Japanese buckler fern) The broadly triangular fronds, are a glossy, coppery pink and they hold this colour until mature.

**D. wallichiana** A conspicuous fern with the

Fig 36 A shaded and effective woodland setting with a meandering path through shade- and moisture-loving plants. A restful planting.

young fronds being a bright golden green. As they mature, the fronds become more green.

**Onoclea sensibilis** (sensitive or bead fern) The light green, ovate fronds are heart-shaped and the plant likes a moist, neutral to acid soil.

## IVIES

There can be few people who do not readily recognize an ivy plant. The very distinctive leaf shapes and its ability to clothe whatever it scrambles over, clinging with the aid of its 'hold fasts', makes it a most useful plant in the garden. One of ivy's many attributes is that it likes to grow in the shade, and once planted in weed-free soil, it needs the minimum of care and attention.

Whilst ivies are generally thought of as climbing plants, which indeed they are, many species and clones make excellent ground cover. Their attributes include a general toughness, close leafage, a spreading habit and in many cases, comparative frost hardiness.

In England, nature has practised using ivy as ground cover, as can be seen by anyone who has taken walks in woodlands, lanes, and along the edges of fields bordered by a not-too-dense copse. The ivy that is usually seen is the common or English ivy, *Hedera helix*, but if one looks at the woodland floor, there will probably also be the larger leaved *Hedera hibernica*, the Irish ivy. This ivy sends out its long runners to carpet the ground completely to the exclusion of annual weeds.

As with so many garden plants, the use of ivy

45

*Fig 37 An arborescent (adult) ivy in flower, used as ground cover in dappled shade beneath tall trees.*

in the garden has been the subject of horticultural fashion and is, at present, enjoying a revival.

## The History of Ivy

According to early writings, it is believed that Osiris, the Egyptian law-giver and god of the dead and afterlife, was associated with ivy. The ivy plant was illustrated in his honour in sculpture and hieroglyphics. Mythologically, ivy has been associated with the Greek god Dionysus and the Roman god Bacchus who, it was said, believed that ivy was able to modify the intoxicating effects of wine. At great feasts, guests wore garlands of ivy and drank from cups decorated with this plant.

Ivy has been known since the writings of Pliny the Elder in 314 BC and in England, garlands of ivy are made at Christmas, and the holly and the ivy are mentioned in many Christmas carols. From early times until well into the Middle Ages a bush of ivy hanging on a pole outside an inn indicated to travellers that the best ale was served there. This sign came to be known as an 'alestake' and is mentioned in Chaucer's *Canterbury Tales*. This custom of hanging a bush of ivy on a pole probably gave rise to the phrase 'good wine needs no bush', or in the modern idiom, a good product needs no advertisement.

The early American settlers, if they knew no other garden plant, were at least able to recognize ivy. By its introduction to cultivation, they extended the range of people who came to know ivy in the New World. The Old World – Europe – is the native habitat of ivy, there being no ivies indigenous to the Americas.

*Hedera helix*, the common English ivy, has a long history as a garden plant. In Victorian times, botanists and plant hunters enjoyed considerable patronage which enabled them to search further afield and visit many areas that were, as yet, unexplored. They were then able to bring home to England new plants to enrich the gardens. From among this rich bounty of treasures, several different ivy species were added to the collections. The introduction of these new varieties so increased their use in Victorian gardens and homes that ivies garlanded windows, door frames, grottoes and monuments. In fact, the Victorians seem to have taken ivy to their hearts by even decorating china, jewellery, linen and the equivalent to our modern notelets. Songs were written about ivy, and decorated ephemera featuring ivy is now the hobby of many collectors who treasure these examples of an earlier era. It is interesting to mention here that the first recorded ivy with variegated leaves dates back to writings of the eighteenth century and we believe that this was a *Hedera helix*.

It is the enthusiastic gardeners, both amateur and professional, who have perpetuated these 'sports' of ivies with widely differing leaf outlines, many with variegated leaves. We owe them a debt of gratitude, for they selected and propagated, exchanging their finds with other interested gardeners, which ensured that these plants were not lost to cultivation. Because of this intense interest, many of the sixty or so ivies that were written about and illustrated by Shirley Hibberd in his book *The Ivy*, published in 1872, are with us to this day.

## Nomenclature and Distribution

There are ten or eleven species of ivy, depending

*Fig 38   Ground cover using various variegated ivies.*

Ivies are available in a wide range of leaf sizes, shapes, textures, colour and growth habits which can enhance or contrast with landscape features. They can be planted for year-round interest as ground cover, in sun or shade, either in groups of single different ivies or a few plants of one cultivar. They can be used to camouflage rock piles or tree stumps and make excellent garden border edgings. Depending upon growth habit and hardiness, miniature ivies can be used in the rock garden or as accent plants, and treated as hardy, evergreen perennials.

In some of the colder areas of England and Europe, ivies can defoliate in the extremes of winter to the point that growth can die down to the ground. Almost invariably, they will appear again the following spring, and are, in this context, considered to be half-hardy perennials. Results of hardiness trials, plus observations from other plantings of ivy enthusiasts, suggest that in England they are far hardier in winter and are more dependable in summer drought and heat than was previously suspected. They therefore deserve wider recognition and use in the landscape.

Ivies have a diversity of appearance from the typical five-lobed ivy to the narrowly lobed, 'bird's foot' outlines. Some ivies are exceedingly curly, some have leaves that are heart shaped or in the shape of fans and some are variegated or multi-coloured according to their seasonal colouring. They can successfully withstand repeated pruning year after year. In the recommendations for planting and care, the two biggest hurdles to overcome when establishing a bed of hardy ground cover is the slowness of growth in the first year of planting and possible winter damage of young plants. It is best to break up the root mass in a pot-grown ivy that is to be planted out, to enable the roots to move into the nearby soil. This helps to prevent the root ball rising out of the soil in winter. The plant should be watered in and should continue to be watered until it is well established.

Usually, very little growth takes place in the first year:

upon the consensus of opinion among botanists. Already mentioned are *Hedera helix* and *H. hibernica* which are indigenous to Britain and Ireland. To these two can be added *H. azorica* from the Azores; *H. colchica*, the Persian ivy; *H. nepalensis*, the Himalayan ivy; *H. pastuchovii*, the Russian ivy; *H. rhombea*, the Japanese ivy and *H. canariensis* which has now been cited by some botanists as an early introduction from North Africa and not from the Canary Islands (*see* page 51). It is now therefore called *H. algeriensis* by many modern botanists. Two other ivy species, *H. caucasigena* and *H. chinensis* might well be added to this list, that is, if botanists decide that these ivies are not variants of existing species.

Thus it can be seen that the various species of ivy cover the globe from Britain in the west to Japan in the east. Interestingly, there are no ivies native to the Americas, Australasia and most of Africa.

Fig 39  Small variegated-leaved ivy making an attractive and effective cover.

Ivy planted in the first year will sleep,
In the second year it creeps
And in the third year it leaps.

Ivies do not need a rich soil and grow equally well whether the soil is acid or alkaline. If you have an area of soil that is in poor heart and you do not wish to spend time and money by digging in fertilizers and humus, then ivy can give a reasonable show for very little expense. However, for success, as with the plantings of any other genus that I have written about in this book, the ground must be free of all perennial weeds.

It is interesting to realize how popular ivy has become in amenity planting. Some years ago, I attended a conference in the north-eastern part of the United States where ivies were being evaluated for their overall vigour and aesthetic qualities in enduring a non-traditional planting site. Other sites chosen for tests were traffic-island beds and along roadways that had facilities for planting beside the pavements. In this latter site, often subject to full sunlight, drying winds and the reflected light from the surrounding asphalt, the results from both types of site seemed to be sufficiently favourable for the Parks and Gardens Department to use ivies more extensively in other areas of roadway environs as well as other municipal plantings. Maintenance, I would add, of these *Hedera helix* cultivars, consisted only of cutting back to the ground in the spring and using balanced fertilizers. Thus ivy for use in certain low-maintenance, high-visibility areas was considered to be a great success.

## Ivy Varieties and Growth Habits

*Hedera hibernica* is a vigorous growing ivy whose stems are green, and whose petioles, or leaf stems, have a purple tinge to the basic green. The leaves are a dull matt green, five lobed with the centre lobe quite large and more prominent with shallow sinuses. The leaves can be quite large, slightly upward folded and can, under good growing conditions, measure 3½×5½in (9×14cm) from the tip to the base of the leaf.

Many European cities and towns contain numerous examples of the value of Irish ivy as a decorative background to splendid buildings and follies. Many celebrated cemeteries, both in England and Europe, have examples of ivy portrayed in carvings on tombstones with the living plant used as ground cover, often close clipped. Unfortunately, many of these cemeteries are not

as well kept today as they were in the early 1900s. *Hedera hibernica* can be seen lining the banks of motorways, freeways and island beds of amenity plantings in parks and gardens, particularly in the city of Seattle, Washington, on the west coast of the United States. I was quite taken aback by the extent of these plantings and the good use to which this ivy had been put, providing trouble-free ground cover. The success of these plantings, I am sure, is due to the climate and amount of rainfall, which is quite comparable to that in England.

*Hedera hibernica* has three variegated forms, one of which is *H.h.* 'Variegata' which Shirley Hibberd called 'Pallida'. This ivy has normal sized *hibernica* leaves of which some are entirely daffodil yellow. The colouring is often defined by a vein, while others have rigidly defined segments that are coloured. This variegation can be quite

*Fig 40   A beech tree with a most attractive fungus,* Polyporus giganteus.

striking, but unfortunately, this plant tends to make a mass of growth of all-green *hibernica* leaves which should be pruned out at least once a year to maintain the attractive appearance.

There is also another clone, *H. hibernica* 'Maculata' which has leaves of three colours, green, grey and white. Such variegation tends to be sparse on an established plant unless the un-

Fig 41   *Two colourful ivies grown in juxtaposition as ground cover.*

wanted, quite strong growth of green leaves are pruned out at least once a year. This will improve the appearance and will encourage the blotched and irregular variegation of the colouring and patterning of the leaves to be seen to advantage. The third clone, and undoubtedly the best, was only very recently selected and distributed amongst ivy enthusiasts. This is *H. hibernica* 'Rona' which was found in 1975, growing in a planting of the ordinary green *hibernica* in the United States National Arboretum. It was found by Rona Schaepman, wife of a former President of the American Ivy Society and was named in her honour. Almost all the leaves are variegated and of a creamy gold colour with an overlay of green freckles and blotches in quite an irregular pattern. The younger leaves are quite dramatic with their contrasting colours, the older leaves taking on more subdued hues. This plant is not such a vigorous grower as the green *hibernica* and is my favourite recommendation for ground cover in areas of dappled shade that are not too wind-blown.

You will find the green-leaved *hibernica* to be readily available in garden centres, but these three variegated clones will need to be sought from specialist nurseries or through contact with members of the British Ivy Society.

**Hedera canariensis 'Gloire de Marengo'**  This is the popular variegated ivy that is seen as a pot plant with quite large ovate leaves which, when well grown, can measure 4×4in(10×10cm). The basic leaf colour is light green with large areas of silvery grey-green and with a yellow and white variegation at the leaf edge. Some of the leaves can be slightly concave, this is due to the greener areas of the leaves growing faster than the silvery grey-green areas which contain less chlorophyll. The stems of the growths and the petioles are a rich wine red colour.

This ivy was found as a sport at an Algerian villa, the Villa Marengo, and is the variegated ivy that has been known for seventy years as the Canary Island ivy. Botanists are now asking us to change the species name to *Hedera algeriensis*. This plant probably entered commerce in the middle 1920s. It is not totally hardy in the severest of winters as it is susceptible to frost damage and searing winds, resulting in the leaves scorching off. However, well-established plants will sprout again from the roots.

Commercial nurserymen world-wide, and particularly in England and America, must have propagated many millions of plants of this ivy to fulfil the demand for house plants. It is accredited in statistics as outselling, by many times, its nearest rival in this field and is said to be not only the most popular pot plant but also to be the most popular ivy as a pot plant.

There is another clone which has sported from *H. canariensis* 'Gloire de Marengo' in which the leaves, in earlier selections, had a maculate appearance, that is, spotted and blotched markings of green over cream in various and irregular widths around the margins of green leaves. However, with the passing of time and reselection, we can now obtain plants of this ivy with leaves that are of a light yellow colour with spots, blotches and splashes of green over the entire leaf. In this form, it is sold in the nursery trade as *Hedera canariensis* 'Maculata', though some authorities still hold with the name 'Margino Maculata' by which the original margined form was known when named in 1942. From a hardiness point of view, this ivy is less frost resistant in cold districts, possibly because of the lack of chlorophyll in the leaves.

There is a good green-leaved form in this species, namely *Hedera canariensis* 'Ravensholst'. This is very vigorous with particularly large, tri-lobed, glossy green leaves which become almost black in winter. These large leaves can measure 6in (15cm) from the tip of the leaf to the truncate base and to nearly as much in width. Again, this ivy still retains the wine-red stems and petioles and is really only suitable for milder areas and sheltered sites.

**Hedera colchica**  In the green form, this is sometimes given the nickname of the 'Elephant's Ears' ivy because its leaves are largely ovate, generally unlobed and can measure as much as 4½×3in(12×8cm). It has a cordate leaf base and the leaves are a dull, dark green. They have a typical odour of celery when crushed. The stems and petioles are green.

The size of those leaves is considerably exceeded by the clone *H. colchica* 'Dentata', the leaves of which can reach, in extremes, 7in (18cm) in length by a little less in width. These leaves are unlobed, roughly heart-shaped with the leaf margins having widely spaced, fine 'teeth'. The leaf colour is a rich, light green and the stems and petioles are a blend of green, purple and brown.

Two excellent variegated clones are *H. colchica* 'Dentata Variegata' and *H. colchica* 'Sulphur Heart'. The first of these was circulated by specialist nurseries from the very early 1900s, and is undoubtedly quite dramatic in that the leaves are almost as big as the green form previously mentioned. The basic leaf colour is light green with irregular patches of grey-green and irregular margin widths of a good yellow. Occasionally, a well-established plant will throw leaves that are part yellow or completely yellow. The leaf texture is leathery with a matt surface and the leaf margins tend to fold under and retain the characteristic, forward-pointing 'teeth'.

*H.c.* 'Sulphur Heart' is a recently selected clone and was a sport that was distributed from Holland just before World War II. This ivy has large, unlobed, cordate leaves of at least 4in (10cm) in length and slightly less in width. The leaf colouring is a rich green with large central, irregular splashes of chartreuse yellow. The stems and petioles are a light green which darken to brown as the growths age. This ivy is sometimes sold under the incorrect name of 'Paddy's Pride'. There is an interesting story behind this name which was given to it by a large nursery. It was first brought to their attention when it was seen growing quite magnificently up the side of a general store in Ampfield, Hampshire. Apparently, the plant had been given as a gift to the store's owner by friends in Holland and, inevitably, as the owner's name was Paddy, the ivy came to be distributed as 'Paddy's Pride'. It can still be found under this erroneous name in some nurseries.

With these larger leaved ivies I recommend that you fashion 12in (30cm) lengths of stout wire into a narrow hoop, rather like the thick hairpins of yester-year. (Lengths of dry cleaners' coat-hangers are excellent sources for this wire.) The use of these hoops will enable you to peg the ivy growths down on to the ground approximately every 2 feet(60cm) to encourage the growths to root into the ground, so anchoring them and preventing them from being blown about by gusts of wind. The increased root growths will enable the plant to draw extra nourishment and extend its ground covering ability.

## Hedera Helix Varieties

Compared with those ivies previously mentioned, the leaves of *Hedera helix* are somewhat smaller, generally measuring no more than 1½–2in (4–5cm) in length and a little less in width. There are many clones to choose from; those that have an artistically sculptured outline with green leaves and many with variegated colourings and patternings that are very attractive. They are ideal for ground cover on the smaller areas of soil that are in sunlight or dappled shade. Plantings of the variegated ivies add an accent of light and colour under trees where little else will grow.

It is this very English ivy, *Hedera helix*, that has so fascinated ivy enthusiasts. In America in the 1920s, a sport occurred which differed from the normal *Hedera helix* in that the leaves were thinner and all growths had lateral side shoots. These ivy plants were said to be 'ramulose', having a much branching habit. It is owing to this 'sporting break' that today we have such a wide choice from over four hundred green and variegated leaved ivies, almost all having been selected for some particular characteristic of growth habit, leaf shape or colour.

Variegated ivies can be obtained with leaves showing combinations of white, cream, yellow, gold, chartreuse and various shades of green and a range of greys. Many of the green-leaved ivies can show attractive winter colouration and many

*Fig 42*   Hedera helix *'Tesselata' making an attractive ground cover in dappled shade. The leaves have a tesselated patterning of variegation.*

of the variegated ivies may take on tints of pink or red.

**Hedera helix 'Anne Marie'**   A most attractive ivy with 2–2½in (5–6cm) leaves that are somewhat wider than long with a white to cream margin and grey-green central markings.

**Hedera helix 'Ardingly'**   The leaves are no larger than 1in (2½cm) and somewhat less in width and have a cream margin to a grey-green centre. This ivy is self-branching, makes a good bushy blanket of cover and is ideal for a sunlit spot.

**Hedera helix 'Atropurpurea'**   This is an old ivy that was recorded in early writings and has a vigorous growth habit. In the summer, the five-lobed leaves are of a dark green and in the winter months they colour to a deep purple, depending upon the degree of exposure to cold weather. It is sometimes seen growing in hedgerows or in the grounds of large estates. This ivy might be found in nurseries as 'Purpurea' or 'Nigra'.

**Hedera helix 'Boskoop'**   This was selected in Holland and has smallish green leaves, somewhat longer than they are wide and which have narrowly cut, forward-facing lobes that cross over one another.

**Hedera helix 'Buttercup'**   An ivy with greenish-yellow new growths and whose mature leaves are quite eye catching. It is best grown in strong light to bring out the intense buttercup-yellow colouring.

*Fig 43* Hedera helix *'Buttercup' growing beneath trees. In this position, the young growths are a particularly attractive yellow colour.*

**Hedera helix 'Caecilia'** An attractive, crinkle edged, cream margined ivy that throws occasional almost pure cream leaves. This is sometimes erroneously offered in nurseries as *H.h.* 'Clotted Cream'.

**Hedera helix 'Caenwoodiana Aurea'** This is a 'bird's foot' ivy and was recorded in the writings of Shirley Hibberd. It needs to be planted in sunlight for, as the leaves mature, they become flushed with a blotched golden hue. The forward facing leaf lobe is considerably extended from the four almost rudimentary lobes at the base of the leaves. This ivy makes an excellent patch of ground cover for small spring bulbs on a rockery and can be easily tidied up by judicious pruning.

**Hedera helix 'Curly Locks'** An ivy with quite large, curly green leaves with tightly fluted edges.

**Hedera helix 'Dealbata'** This is a long vining ivy recorded in nineteenth century writings. The young leaves are cream to white, overlaid with irregular green spots and splashes. The three-lobed leaves are of a triangular to arrow shape and when mature, become entirely green and are quite shiny. An ideal ivy to grow in the wilder parts of the garden.

**Hedera helix 'Deltoidea'** The almost entirely lobeless leaves are quite thick in comparison with other *Hedera helix* clones and have a deltoid or heart-shaped outline. The winter colouring is a good bronze-purple. In America, this is sold as the 'Sweetheart' ivy.

**Hedera helix 'Dragon Claw'** The large five to six lobed, light-green leaves are very curly and have tightly fluted edges which are most attractive.

54

**Hedera helix 'Glacier'** This is one of the earliest variegated ivies selected from the 'ramulose' sporting. The leaves are three to five lobed of roughly 1½–2in (3–5cm) and are of a mixture of grey and green with lighter silver-grey patches and a very thin cream rim. It can throw variously shaped leaves and mixtures of colour and is quite hardy in most parts of the country.

**Hedera helix 'Glymii'** The fairly small, deep-green leaves are very glossy and in the winter take on a rich purple colouring.

**Hedera helix 'Ivalace'** The very dark-green, shiny and curly leaves are quite small, measuring about ¾–1in (2–3cm) long. The crimped edges give a lace-like appearance.

**Hedera helix 'Königer's Auslese'** This makes a bushy plant and has deeply indented green leaves the shape of which resemble a bird's foot. It can blanket an area, rooting as it goes, which makes it most useful to use as ground cover.

**Hedera helix 'Lalla Rookh'** A large, curly, green leaved ivy with deeply cut and toothed leaves.

**Hedera helix 'Lemon Swirl'** A good, self-branching clone. The leaves are sparsely toothed and measure no more than 1×1in (2.5×2.5cm). When grown in sunlight, many of the leaves are brightly flushed yellow.

*Fig 44 An amalgum of ivy ground cover, the bright leaves of* Hedera helix *'Lemon Swirl' can be quite eye catching even from a distance.*

**Hedera helix 'Manda Crested'** This is quite a beautiful ivy whose mature leaves can measure as much as 2×2in (5×5cm) and are gently curled. This makes an attractive curly ground cover, resembling waves rolling on a sandy beach. Young growths at the tips are often flushed with a rich pink.

**Hedera helix 'Maple Leaf'** This ivy was a selection by a German enthusiast and has attractive leaves which are six lobed and highly toothed with a lacy appearance, very much resembling the cut leaved forms of Japanese maples.

**Hedera helix 'Midas Touch'** This is a quite recent introduction from Denmark having quite rich golden leaves which are overlaid with largish splashes of deep green. The leaf outline is irregular with quite rudimentary lobes, though the leaf is not quite entire. It has surprisingly proved to be quite hardy and seems not to suffer from scorch in sunlight. As the original introduction to this country was unnamed, I registered this ivy in the name of 'Midas Touch'.

**Hedera helix 'Minor Marmorata'** A long vining ivy that was recorded in Shirley Hibberd's book 'The Ivy'. Its new growth with smallish, creamy white leaves are overlaid with green and grey speckles. The more mature leaves are quite green and show little or no speckling. This ivy is sometimes offered erroneously as *H.h.* 'Discolor' by older established nurseries who are reluctant to bring their plant nomenclature up to date.

**Hedera helix 'Ritterkreuz'** An excellently textured, green leaved ivy with the shape of the individual leaves resembling a Maltese Cross. This too, is a German introduction, adding to the vast numbers of named and registered clones.

**Hedera helix 'Spetchley'** This is probably the smallest-leaved ivy and has, at times, been called by nurserymen. *H.h.* 'Minima'. The dark green leaves are three-lobed, the centre lobe being quite elongated. The stems and petioles are a good purple. This is ideal for use in rockeries and very suitable for growing between paving stones.

**Hedera helix 'Succinata'** An ivy with small, typical three-lobed green leaves which are wider than they are long. In dappled shade and sunlight, the leaves take on an amber colouring with a quite noticeably suffused pink tinge which becomes more pronounced in extreme winter temperatures. The name 'Succinata' is derived from the Latin word for amber, *succinum*. This cultivar was called the amber leaved ivy by Shirley Hibberd in his book *The Ivy* in 1872.

This ivy has been grown and propagated particularly in Holland, by many generations of nurserymen who have distributed it erroneously as *H.h.* 'Buttercup'.

**Hedera helix 'Tricolor'** A long vining, slow growing ivy with purple petioles to the leaves which are triangular, mostly unlobed, with an irregular cream edge and a grey-green centre. The leaf margins have a thin pink edge which suffuses further into the leaf in winter months. The intensity of this pink colouring is often remarked upon when attention is drawn to it during that period.

**Hedera helix 'Woerner'** A vigorous growing, green-leaved ivy with quite large leaves for a *helix*. However, the interest with this ivy is that its leaves take on a rich purple colour in winter.

Ivy is a plant of infinite variety. There are many more *helix* clones that you may come across, with or without names, in the garden centres or nurseries. The plants are often offered in small pots and will have been grown on to a saleable size in tunnels or greenhouses. Unless the weather is suitable, and certainly not earlier than May, I recommend that they are not planted out immediately as they will need some degree of hardening off before planting, having originally been intended for use as pot plants in the home.

In preparing these plants for outside extremes of wind and temperature, they should be put into shade and out of the wind for several weeks, gradually moving the pots to a more exposed location. Never put indoor-grown plants into direct sunlight without them first being acclimatized in the manner that I have recommended. Plant the ivy at the same level as when it was potted, gently separate and spread the roots in the planting hole and keep watered until the plant is well established. Because future generations deserve to inherit the beauty and diversity of ivy, take cuttings from established plants to propagate, which will increase your plant stock and provide you with extra plants to exchange with other ivy enthusiasts.

## HERBS

Ideally, an area for a herb garden should be nearer to the kitchen than to the bottom of the garden, where it could be very inconvenient if you were in the process of making a stir-fry or a complicated sauce.

The herbs need to be grown in sunlight or dappled shade and a well-drained area is essential. The ground should be free of all perennial weeds before planting and the soil thoroughly enriched with a good dressing of proprietary fertilizer or an organic, slow-release fertilizer such as blood, fish and bone-meal. After planting, a dressing of high potash fertilizer applied annually will help to keep the plants hardy. Nitrogen fertilizers should be avoided as they encourage soft growth which then becomes prone to winter damage.

Herbs need not be grown in isolation; many people make a feature of a herb bed and have chosen a patch where different herbs are grown

Fig 45 Ruta graveolens *provides a variation in the green range, adding a glaucous hue.*

cheek by jowl. Very often though, this is an area that is not entirely suitable because the soil is poor and in shade with heavy soil that is not well drained. Sometimes, it can be the area where the dustbin is kept or where there are funnelling winds between the garage and house wall.

There is a great revival of interest in growing and using herbs. This could be because people are becoming tired of bland, mass-produced food, preferring more interesting flavours. The planting of herbs seems to fit in with the current fashion for cottage gardens, and they provide material not only for cooking, but also for pot-pourri, herbal medicine and beauty products.

## Designing a Herb Garden

The shape of the herb bed may be a basic half-circle or indeed any shape that fits in the area that is available. It should be planted somewhat like a small herbaceous border, with herbs planted in graduation according to plant heights, the lower growing plants in the front and the taller plants behind them. However, this design necessitates walking between the plants and on to the soil, which, on an inclement day, can be an uninviting prospect.

Some designed gardens have a herb wheel and usually this is an old cartwheel with different herbs planted in each section. However, if the wheel is placed in the centre of a flower bed, it may be still necessary to walk on the earth if paving has not been placed around the wheel. In addition, cartwheels are hard to come by today and the wood will rot in a few years even though the wheel might have been painstakingly prepared and painted before being laid on the ground.

In many larger suburban gardens, garden designers have reproduced the cartwheel theme by using bricks laid in a circle with brick paths of a one-brick width radiating from the centre. Where the spokes meet, a gap can be left and a tall plant such as rosemary can be planted there. This is a far more enduring, practical

*Fig 46   The cartwheel used for growing different herbs between the spokes.*

Fig 47   The stylized cartwheel using brick.

and attractive idea and is another aspect of planting for ground cover.

The cottage gardener of yester-year often had a herb path made of crazy paving, and a mass of low-growing thyme, with the taller herbs set on either side of this pathway.

## A Herb Chess Board

With the principal aim of having a clean, dry footing which will allow you to reach each of the herbs, I suggest that 12×12in (30×30cm) paving stones are laid out in the pattern of a chess or draughts board. That is to say, that the 'black' squares should be the planting holes and the 'white' squares the dry hard stand. The number of paving slabs needed and the number of planting holes can be judged according to the size of the garden and the amount of space available.

## Choosing the Herbs

This will obviously be a matter for personal preference but bear in mind that the selection should be based on culinary requirements as well as those of horticulture, that is to say, those plants that are grown for decorative purposes. Many common herbs are annuals or perennials which will die down completely in the winter. Quite a few herbs are native to warmer climates than ours and can lose most of their leaves in all but the mildest of winters.

Do remember that a dry, hard stand or pathway will enable you to reach each and every herb that you may require, and that the area you have chosen will only be able to accommodate a certain number of plants. Select the herbs that appeal to you and those that you are likely to use most often.

Most garden centres and nurseries have a herb section, but for a wider choice, visit a specialist herb nursery where there will possibly be a more unusual selection. There is a diversity of leaf colour in herbs, from the blue of thyme to the pink flowers of chives and the fresh, lush green of parsley.

The most usual choice of herbs is parsley, sage, rosemary, mint, and thyme and I would like to

59

*Fig 48   The draught-board effect with 12×12in (30×30cm) paving slabs.*

suggest that you include dill, fennel, chervil, lovage, basil and sorrel. There is the French sorrel, *Rumex scutatus* and you may care to look for *R.s.* 'Silver Shield' which has very decorative silver coloured leaves. This plant will accept being planted in some shade but does not like extreme cold and badly drained soil. The bitter, slightly lemony flavour of the leaves is due to their oxalic acid content and this adds a refreshing sharpness to the otherwise bland flavours of lettuce and cucumber.

There are many different mints, offering a wide variety of foliage colour and aromas, including eau-de-Cologne, apple, lemon, pineapple, peppermint and ginger.

The apple mint, *Mentha × rotundifolia* 'Variegata' has lovely white and green leaves with a frilly edge, whilst the ginger mint, *Mentha ×*

*gentilis* 'Aurea' has leaves that are streaked with yellow. The peppermint-scented mint *Mentha × piperata* has leaves that are a dark green, similar to those of the common mint, and some varieties have leaves that are quite downy.

Please be warned that all mints are extremely invasive and should be planted in a bottomless plastic or metal bucket or similar container to prevent their roots from wandering.

A bay tree (*Laurus nobilis*) is best grown in a tub as it is inclined to be tender. Grown in this way it can be moved to shelter in winter in the colder areas. The dark, shining leaves are most attractive and are a must for culinary use. There is also a golden leaved form and both are worth trying in reasonably sheltered gardens.

Plants of rosemary can grow quite tall and may become leggy if not pruned back each year.

*Fig 49* Origanum, *the golden marjoram.*

Several sprigs sprinkled on a joint when cooking roast lamb give a delicious flavour.

Sage, winter savoury and hyssop are semi-evergreen, whilst the ever-useful common thyme has many species and clones with differing aromatic scents and flavours. Some have golden leaves and others have silver variegated leaves. There are four or five coloured-leaved forms of sage and a specialist nursery would, no doubt, be able to offer these.

The leaves of lemon balm, *Melissa officinalis* can be used instead of lemon peel in soups and stews, fruit salad and cooked rhubarb, salads and omelettes. The fresh leaves can also be used as a garnish for summer drinks which adds a distinct lemon touch. There is an all-golden leaved form, *Melissa officinalis* 'All Gold', which is quite attractive, and another form whose leaves are only partly gold. All will grow to 2–3 feet (0.60–1

metre). All flower heads should be cut off as soon as they appear, otherwise there will be an excess of seedlings starting to grow in and among other plants.

Other fragrant herbs include bergamot, *Monarda*, which has attractive, colourful flowers and fragrant leaves.

The curry plant, *Helichrysum angustifolium*, has silvery leaves and makes a small shrub. In the summer, the area surrounding the plant smells of curry.

Lavenders, *Lavandula sp.*, are well known for their fragrance. There are many forms such as 'Hidcote' a good blue. 'Hidcote Pink' with pink flowers and 'Jackman's Dwarf'. There are white-flowered forms and a particularly interesting dwarf white form is 'Nana Alba'. For the name alone, seek out 'Twickel Purple'.

Scented-leaved pelargoniums are tender, but if

*Fig 50*  Choisya ternata *making a good, bright contrast leading to the lavender.*

planted in their pots in the summer and put into the ground, they can then be lifted and housed in a frost-free greenhouse in the winter. They are particularly attractive and their fragrance can be appreciated when the leaves are bruised.

The last three plants mentioned are useful for inclusion in a scented area of the garden.

Basil or sweet basil, (*Ocimum basilicum*) is essential for culinary use in Italian dishes, in tomato salad and in soups.

Borage, (*Borago officinalis*) is an annual with very pretty blue flowers. A sprig of this is very pleasant in summer drinks and the flowers, if frozen in an ice cube and then used in drinks, can be a delightful addition. The flowers can also be used to decorate a serving of ice cream or sorbet for a special dinner or luncheon party. I grow a variegated form which comes partly true from seed but this is not yet available commercially.

## ROSES

There have been available for some many years now, roses that have a sprawling, scrambling growth habit and which will carpet the soil and ultimately provide an area that is totally weed free. In more recent times, several rose breeders have been able to select roses that are specifically bred and described in their catalogues as 'ground cover roses'. In America, growers have bred roses which they call 'carpeting roses'. However, as can well be imagined, until the roses have made sufficient growth, there will be uncomfortable difficulty in removing wind-blown seeds that have germinated.

It cannot be stressed too strongly that where roses are to be planted, the ground must be absolutely clean beforehand. Once the roses are in, it would be extremely difficult and nigh on

*Fig 51 A kaleidoscopic waterside planting.*

impossible to remove perennial weeds such as couch grass, ground elder and bindweed. There are roses that tend to arch and entwine with one another eventually providing a totally impenetrable thicket of ground cover which will stay weed free and repel all boisterous animals. These roses are for the wilder areas of your garden and can be extensively used for planting on sloping banks in well-drained soil and essentially in full sun. These prostrate growers creep along the ground horizontally and can have a growth spread of 3 feet (1 metre) or more across. The really rampant growers can reach 10–12 feet (4 metres) across and are obviously for use in the larger gardens. Little or no pruning will be required although excessive pruning will encourage a more vigorous growth but will reduce the amount of flowers produced.

The late Margery Fish of East Lambrook Manor, Somerset, one of the great gardeners of our time, was a real plantswoman who recommended the pegging down of the long trails of hybrid perpetual roses, particularly in areas around early flowering trees and shrubs. She proved that many of these roses flowered more profusely when pegged down than when grown in the upright position, when often flowers only came at the end of the stems.

She was very fond of a white rose 'Frau Karl Druschki' and also 'Hugh Dickson' which has bright scarlet-crimson flowers. In her plantings at East Lambrook, 'Souvenir du Docteur Jamain' which has dark, velvety flowers of a purplish crimson, was grown in a shady part of the garden and when pegged down, had the advantage of flowering for a second time in the autumn, though to do this, the rose needs a good, rich soil.

Old friends and faithful, 'American Pillar' and 'Dorothy Perkins' are easy to train along the ground. The pastel pink 'New Dawn', 'Alberic Barbier' with creamy white flowers, 'Albertine' with copper pink flowers, together with 'Dr van Fleet' with silver pink flowers, the latter having brilliant red shoots as an added attraction, are also excellent subjects for the pegging down method.

Margery Fish's garden is still being maintained and is well worth a visit if you are in the area.

The rose that can be used for ground cover without any assistance from the gardener is *Rosa wichuraiana* which grows very close to the ground and makes a close carpet of small, shiny leaves, and does very well in a light, sandy soil. Its small flowers are of a pale cream colour. I recommend that you seek out the variegated form of this rose for its leaves have the attraction of a white variegation. The young leaves are suffused pink and the young shoots are of a good, cerise pink colour. This is sometimes offered in specialist nurseries, quite erroneously, as *Rosa wichuraiana* 'Variegata minor'. The 'minor', I think, has been added by nurserymen who propagate this rose on its own roots and offer them for sale in small 3in (7cm) pots as a novelty. In good soil, and over a number of years, this plant will make an excellent and attractive splash of colour at the edge of a rock garden or at the edges of flower borders where the lush growth of perennial plants are not likely to smother it.

The roses listed below with their brief descriptions will help you to make your selection.

## The Prostrate Growers

**R. 'Grouse'** This shrub rose grows to about 10 feet (3 metres) wide but only a few inches high. In July–August, there are single, fragrant, pale-pink blooms borne in profusion and the glossy, mid-green foliage is disease resistant.

**R. 'Max Graf'** A vigorous, prostrate grower and is a hybrid rugosa rose. It will reach to 6 feet (2 metres) or more across and 18in (46cm) in height. The flowers are single, bright pink with a lighter centre and appear in June–July.

**R. 'Nozomi'** This is a climbing miniature rose bearing large clusters of pearly pink, single flowers. Its gently arching sprays growing up to 4 feet(1.3 metres) across makes a pretty ground covering shrub.

**R. 'Pheasant'** This is a spectacular variety growing up to 2 feet (60cms) high and 10 feet (3 metres) or more across. The large, full blooms of a deep rose pink are borne in trusses on the vigorous prostrate growth.

**R. 'Pink Drift'** A rose with handsome foliage on the prostrate growth which can reach to 10 feet (3 metres) across but will be less than 1 foot (30cm) high. The small, pale-pink double flowers are borne in large clusters.

**R. 'Red Max Graf'** The arching growth of this prostrate shrub rose can reach to 5 feet (1.50 metres) or more and bears clusters of large, single, bright scarlet flowers.

**R. 'Paulii'** This is a large sprawling shrub whose massed stems, arching over each other, make a dense thicket and a smothering ground cover. It can grow to 4 feet (1.3 metres) or more in height and 12 feet (4 metres) in breadth. Flowering in July, the starry, white flowers are richly scented.

**R. 'Snow Carpet'** A prostrate grower with a compact habit, therefore rather more of a miniature ground coverer. It will grow to about 6in (15cm) high and about 3 feet (1 metre) in breadth, producing pure white, small double flowers from June until October.

## The Arching and Bushy Growers

These arching shrubs can reach 3 feet (1 metre) or more in height but will be considerably more in width. The lower growth hugs the ground and will smother weeds in the same manner as the prostrate growers.

**R. 'Bonica'** This arching shrub forms a good ground cover when densely planted, each plant growing to about 3×3 feet (1×1 metre). When fully open, the pale-pink flowers deepen in colour.

**R. 'Ferdy'** The arching growth makes a wide, spreading bush 4 feet (1.3 metres) wide and 3 feet (1 metre) high. The soft, fuchsia-pink, double flowers open to show creamy yellow centres.

**R. 'Fiona'** The arching shoots on this bush bear trusses of semi-double, blood-red blooms. The growth can reach 4–5 feet (1.50 metres) wide and 3 feet (1 metre) high.

**R. 'Hansa'** This very fragrant and free-flowering rose has double flowers of reddish-violet, followed by large red hips. It makes good ground cover as the growth can reach 3 feet (1 metre).

**R. 'Pink Bells'** Of an arching, spreading habit, this rose will grow to about 4 feet (1.3 metres) wide and reach 2 feet 6 inches (0.76 metres) in height. The small, neat leaves are a shiny dark green and the large clusters of soft pink full blooms are borne throughout July and August.

**R. 'Pink Wave'** A vigorous arching shrub which will grow to 4 feet (1.3 metres) wide and up to 3 feet (1 metre) high. The soft satin pink double blooms appear in great profusion from June and through September.

**R. 'Red Blanket'** This rose makes dense growth and has a strong, arching habit. Small, semi-double, rose-red flowers are borne throughout the season. The growth can be 5 feet (1.50 metres) wide and 2–3 feet (0.70–1 metre) in height.

**R. 'Scarlet Mediland'** The glossy, disease resistant foliage on the arching growth which can reach to 3 feet (1 metre) high and spread to 4–5 feet (1.50 metres) across, bears clusters of orange-red blooms.

**R. 'The Fairy'** A repeat flowering rose with small double soft-pink flowers on a 2–3 feet (0.60–1 metre) high bush, spreading to a breadth of 4 feet (1.2 metres).

**R. 'White Bells'** This has the same growth habit as 'Pink Bells' but has delightful white flowers.

Ground cover roses are lovely in their own right and fit into all sizes and styles of garden. The following selection are roses that have been recently bred specifically for ground cover and are repeat flowering from June until late October. The smaller growing, miniature types are particularly suitable for the rockery and patio garden, whilst others, of more vigorous growth, will do well in covering unsightly or under-used areas in the garden, providing that such areas are in sunlight.

One particular breeder's selection is called 'The County Series':

**R. 'Essex'**  This rose bears rich pink flowers in large clusters. The low dense growth has small glossy leaves with even spreading shoots and grows to about 2 feet (60cm) high and 4 feet (1.3 metres) in width.

**R. 'Hampshire'**  This is a dense shrub growing to about 1 foot (30cm) high by 2 feet (60cm) wide and is covered with single blooms throughout summer and autumn. The petals of glowing scarlet have a central crown of gold stamens which are followed in autumn with orange-red hips.

**R. 'Kent'**  A compact little shrub rose, bearing semi-double blooms of pure white in great profusion. Unlike many other roses of this colour, the flowers will withstand any cold, wet summer weather without too much damage.

**R. 'Norfolk'**  The first yellow ground cover rose with very fragrant, double blooms. These are borne in clusters on a neat bushy plant which will grow to about 18 inches (46cm) high by 2 feet (60cm) wide.

**R.** **'Northamptonshire'**  A ground-hugging shrub making growth of about 18 inches (46cm) high by 3 feet (1 metre) wide which has been awarded a Certificate of Merit by the Royal National Rose Society. The dense growth bears flesh-pink and white blooms that are a perfect buttonhole shape.

**R. 'Rutland'**  The glossy, dark green foliage of this ground-hugging little bush will grow to about 1 foot (30cm) high. The flowers are much like the simple dog rose of the English hedgerows. These are a soft pink and will bloom from June until the first frosts.

**R. 'Suffolk'**  A low spreading shrub of 18 inches (46cm) in height and 3 feet (1 metre) across, bearing blooms of brilliant scarlet with prominent golden stamens. Orange-red hips follow in the autumn.

**R. 'Surrey'**  This is a wide spreading shrub rose of 2–3 feet (0.60–1 metre) in height and up to 4 feet (1.3 metres) across. The blooms that are borne in great profusion are double, of a soft pink with a deeper rose colour within the centre of the flowers. This rose flowers throughout the season until the first frosts of autumn.

Also available from another grower are these recent introductions:

**R. 'Eyeopener'**  Ground hugging. A vigorous and spreading rose with healthy, dense foliage, an excellent plant for weed control. The bright-red flowers have a yellow-white eye and prominent golden stamens.

**R. 'Partridge'**  Ground hugging. A rose that has a similar growth habit to the above. The pure white flowers, which are strongly perfumed, are carried in great swathes, so effective against the dark, glossy foliage.

**R. 'Sea Foam'**  Ground hugging. The double white-cream flowers are produced in bunches on a vigorous bush. This rose would make a wonderful display when grown on a bank or trailing over a wall. The glossy foliage appears to be disease resistant.

**R. 'Smarty'**  Ground cover. This robust ground cover rose has single flowers of pale blush pink that are borne continuously throughout the growing season. Its vigorous spreading habit make it an ideal choice for an unsightly or neglected area.

*Fig 52   A bold planting of* Phlox *with roses, backed by a variegated* Aralia.

**R. 'Snow Carpet'**   Miniature ground cover. An unusual rose with dainty, creamy-white flowers that smother the prostrate growth that has miniature leaves of dark olive green. The dense, outward growth will cover 3 feet (1 metre) in width and 9–10in (25cm) in height.

**R. 'Suma'**   Miniature ground cover. This has tiny, glossy green leaves with rosette type red flowers. These continue to bloom in profusion right through the summer and autumn.

**R. 'Tall Story'**   Ground cover. The long sweeping branches of this shrub rose bears strongly scented, pale-primrose flowers continuously from summer to autumn. The hardy, healthy

67

growth is very suitable for the low-maintenance areas in the garden.

As most nurseries and garden centres cannot stock all the 2,500 varieties of roses that are grown in this country, The Rose Growers Association have produced a booklet *Find That Rose* which lists by name the roses that are grown by each of its seventy-seven Association members. Some of the larger garden centres and nurseries may have this booklet for sale in their book section, otherwise it can be obtained from the Editor, *Find That Rose*, 302 Mile End Road, Colchester, Essex CO4 5EA. This guide is updated each year.

## Preparing the Ground for Planting

There are some salient points to follow when preparing the ground for planting roses. The most important point to stress, as I have mentioned elsewhere in this book, is to ensure that the ground is weed free, particularly from the persistent and perennial, deep-rooted weeds.

Roses are at their best when they have a good rich soil in which to grow and this can vary from light sand to heavy clay. It must be remembered that roses are gross feeders, therefore they must be fed well. If you bear in mind that roses dislike cold, wet and boggy soils and do not grow well when planted under trees, then you will have some idea of the growing conditions that they do like. An exception to this is that some roses can put on a fine display when growing in dappled shade.

As with any other plant, roses do not give of their best when they are subjected to funnel draughts which are caused by prevailing winds driving through the narrow apertures between buildings, or on the corners of houses.

It is usually best to prepare the soil for planting from November through to March, provided that there are suitable and conducive weather conditions. A new bed should be well dug and a liberal amount of farmyard manure or compost dug in and mixed well with the soil.

If you have ordered your roses by direct mail or have purchased them from garden centres, it is possible that the weather will not be suitable to plant them immediately. To keep the roses in prime condition, they should be heeled in to a shallow trench until the weather has improved. That is, when all-day frosts and very wet conditions are not prevailing.

When conditions are right to plant the roses, be sure that the hole that has been dug for each rose is sufficiently large for the rose roots to be spread out. The hole should then be filled with a mixture of soil which has been enriched with one of the many proprietary brands of rose fertilizer. To make up your own planting mixture, use a large handful of sterilized bone-meal together with a large bucketful of moist horticultural peat. Gently tread the soil around the roots of your planted rose, topping with the soil that you have dug out of the hole.

It is important that the rose is planted with the union of the stock on the rose just below ground level. In almost all instances, this point can be judged by the mark left from the level of the soil where the rose was grown in the nursery. A stick or plank placed across the planting hole, with your new rose in position, will indicate the height at which this union should be in the planting hole (*see* Fig 53).

## After-Care

Roses should be fed regularly twice in the year, in the spring and again just before the first flush of flower in early summer. Ideally, well-rotted farm-yard manure and well-made garden compost, with the addition of small quantities of fish, blood and bone organic fertilizer make the best mulches for feeding rose beds. These mulches have the added advantage of smothering weeds and conserving moisture.

There are proprietary brands of special rose fertilizers available from the garden centre or nursery which, if sprinkled over the soil and watered in with a hose or a watering can fitted with a fine rose, can produce excellent results.

Fig 53 Planting instructions. (a) You will need a spade, watering can, peat, general fertilizer; (b) ensure that the plant is still moist; (c) mix together equal parts of moist peat and sand and add a little general fertilizer; (d) dig a hole big enough to hold the plant and line the hole with the prepared mixture; (e) place a cane across the hole to check if it is deep enough; the soil surface in the pot should be about 1in (2.5cm) below the cane; (f) remove the plant from the pot and put the plant in position; (g) fill in the space around the plant with compost mixture and firm it down; (h) leave a dip around the plant and water it in well, keeping it regularly watered until established.

Such proprietary brands of fertilizer often contain a mixture, in varying proportions, of blood, fish and bone-meal. However, it must be appreciated that these fertilizers do not add any humus to the soil.

## GREY AND SILVER PLANTS FOR GROUND COVER

When planning the planting of your ground cover, consider using plants that have grey and silver foliage. For those that have hot, and there fore often dry, well-drained soils, this group of plants with a range of silver, white, grey or glaucous foliage could prove useful. Most of these plants have been introduced from their native habitats where, owing to extreme heat they have evolved these forms of colouration to prevent water loss and to survive despite the lack of rainfall, periods of very hot weather or extreme winds.

A close look at grey or silver leaves will reveal that the plants are very hairy, which slows down their water loss in a number of ways. They will grow at their best in an open position and on a

*Fig 54  Silver plants par excellence. A dramatic grouping placed for summer effect.*

well-drained site. Many are hardy and have a good degree of resistance to frost providing that they are grown in conditions that they like. These include the correct planting position, regular pruning to keep the plants compact and not subjected to excessive winter rain.

When plants are purchased from garden centres and selected specialist nurseries, they will already be potted up and can be planted at almost any time of the year. However, the best month in Britain could well be May, after the on/off wet weather has, perhaps, settled down. Some of the tougher 'greys and silvers' can be planted in the autumn.

While many of these plants will put up with very dry conditions once established, it is essential to make sure that there is enough moisture available until they have done this. As a further bonus, they grow very well on alkaline soils that are poor as long as they are never waterlogged. Providing that the soil is well drained, those of you with neutral or even slightly acid soil can have success with growing some of these plants. The majority of greys and silvers are not gross feeders and this is important to remember, as some, if planted in rich soil, will lose their character, become gross and leggy and will succumb to the first frosts or excessive wet weather.

If the basic drainage is poor, all is not lost, as raised beds can be constructed and quantities of sharp horticultural grit dug in; even small, washed pea gravel can be used. Better still, if you have a site that is raised above the level of the surrounding area, providing that this is not a heavy clay, free drainage can be achieved by using the available fall from the high ground to the level of the surrounding area.

With grey and silver ground cover plants, bear in mind that some can be very fast growing and if, in the early stages of growth, they threaten to overwhelm their neighbours, do not be afraid to prune them in order to encourage bushy growth. Pruning can be started on established plants from the end of April and certainly should be done immediately after flowering.

Generally speaking, most grey and silver plants

will stand a fairly hard pruning; I have heard many gardeners complain that such plants are untidy and unattractive. This untidiness of growth is almost invariably due to the neglect of the gardener who has failed to prune adequately. If in doubt, remove over half of the current season's growth immediately after flowering.

## Selected Plant List

All the plants that are listed are hardy and all enjoy hot, dry and well-drained soil conditions.

### Acaena

**Acaena adscendens** An evergreen perennial with pinnate, glaucous grey-green leaves, pink flushed trailing stems and red flowers in late spring. This is a good ground cover plant that can be pruned hard when necessary.

**A. buchananii** Has pale silver green leaves.

**A. 'Blue Haze'** Has glaucous pinky-blue pinnate leaves with red stems.

**A. microphylla** Has leaves that can vary from a greyish to reddish colour.

### Achillea

**Achillea argentea** An evergreen perennial with narrow, slightly serrated grey leaves rising from mat-building rosettes. Clusters of small, white daisy flowers appear in May–June.

**A. × kolbiana** Has short, rounded and divided grey leaves, rosette forming with white daisy flowers.

**A. × kellereri** This is a clump forming evergreen perennial with long, grey, narrow feathery leaves. The flowers are white and are borne on fairly long stems.

**A. 'Moonshine'** Has bold, fern-like, grey leaves and flowers of a soft yellow.

**A. 'Schwallenburg'** Has fern-like leaves that are almost white and flowers of a mid-yellow.

## Alyssum

**Alyssum saxatile**   The narrow grey leaves of this evergreen perennial, common yellow alyssum, form bold clumps and the plant produces numerous heads of bright yellow flowers appearing in the springtime.

**A.s.** 'Citrinum'   This variety is similar to the above but the flowers are a cool lemon yellow.

**A.s.** 'Dudley Neville'   This is again similar, but with flowers of a faded apricot colour. There is a variegated leaved form, *A.s.* 'Dudley Neville Variegated'.

**A.s.** 'Flore Pleno'   This is a more compact plant with bright yellow, double flowers.

**A. montanum** has a prostrate growth habit with steel-grey evergreen leaves on trailing stems. There are clusters of yellow flowers in spring.

**A. stribrnyi**   This is a miniature alyssum that forms a small evergreen clump. The small white leaves and stems are topped with small clusters of bright yellow flowers in spring.

## Anthemis

**Anthemis cupaniana**   The evergreen, filigree foliage will be whitish-grey if grown in a poor, dry soil but tends to be greener if grown in rich soil. White ox-eye daisy flowers appear from mid-spring onwards and again in the autumn.

**A. tuberculata**   This is very similar to the above but with a more compact habit.

**A. rudolphiana** (syn *A. biebersteinii*; *A. marschalliana*) This has slim, feathery grey leaves arising from a dense clump. Bright golden yellow daisy flowers appear in May–June.

## Atennaria

**Atennaria aprica**   An evergreen perennial that has flat mats of rosettes, narrow grey leaves and buff-apricot flowers in May. *A.a. rosea* is a pink

flowered form and *A. diocia rosea* has leaves that give a green- and silver-rimmed effect and rosy pink flowers in May.

## Artemisia

Some can be rather tall in growth for carpeting plants, but are very attractive and worth including, particularly for their aromatic foliage.

**A. brachyloba**   This plant, with its fine, filigree grey foliage and trailing stems, is good when grown to hang over walls. It can be pruned hard in late spring.

**A. caucasica** (syn *A. assoana*; *A. pedemontana*) Has grey foliage and is very good for planting in a rockery.

**A. gracilis**   Has grey feathery leaves and is of a mat forming habit.

**A. schmidtiana**   This plant produces a dome of fine, lacy silvery foliage and revels in a sunny position. It can be trimmed back when it becomes untidy and it will die down completely in the winter months.

**A. stelleriana**   This plant grows in a mat-like form with white, felted, chrysanthemum-like leaves. It can be pruned hard in spring if it becomes untidy. There is a prostrate form, *A.s. prostrata* which is similar, but lower growing and more compact.

**Aubrieta 'Astolat'**   The cream and grey-green variegated leaves produce mats of foliage suitable for planting in the rock garden. In late spring, this will be covered with pale lilac-blue flowers.

**Centaurea simplicicaulis**   This small knapweed has greyish silver divided leaves which arise from rosettes, the solitary flowers are deep pink. *C. stricta* is mat forming with silvery lobed leaves and solitary bright blue flowers in early summer.

**Cerastium tomentosum**   This is a mat forming, creeping plant commonly known as 'snow in

*Fig 55* Hakonechloa macra *'Alboaurea' with* Artemisia *makes a wonderful colour contrast.*

summer'. The silvery leaves are topped with white flowers in mid-summer.

**Cistus salviifolius**   A low spreading, evergreen shrub with grey, sage-like leaves. A profusion of small white sun roses with yellow basal marking appear in mid-summer.

**Crepis incana**   A pink dandelion with typical greyish-green leaves and has masses of pale-pink flowers in mid-summer. A very good plant for the rock garden or the front of a border.

**Dicentra 'Stuart Boothman' (syn 'Boothman's Variety')**   This is a good border plant with finely divided steel grey-pink tinged foliage which remains attractive after the rose-red and pink flowers have died down in early summer. It is best planted in a site that does not dry out completely.

**Helianthemum 'Wisley Pink'**   A superb evergreen rock rose with soft grey foliage and bright pink flowers which is most attractive. It can be pruned hard immediately after flowering.

73

*H.* 'Wisley Primrose' is a primrose-yellow flowering form and *H.* 'Wisley White' is a white-flowered form.

## Helichrysum

**Helichrysum italicum** (syn. H. angustifolium) This is known as the curry plant and is a small shrub with silvery grey, needle-like leaves which have a strong smell of curry in hot weather. The tufts of yellow daisy-like flowers appear in mid-summer. There are more dwarf forms available which are worth looking for.

**H. milfordiae** This has flat, evergreen rosettes of woolly leaves that form a spreading mat. In late spring, there are clusters of paper-white flowers.

*H.* 'Sulphur Light' A low-growing, but slightly more tender form than the above. The narrow, white woolly foliage forms prostrate mats and the flowers are a bright sulphur yellow.

**Hieracium villosum** This woolly leaved hawk-weed has attractive foliage and yellow dandelion-like flowers.

**Hypericum cerastioides** The grey glaucous leaves form a mound, covered in May with small, bright yellow, typical *Hypericum* flowers. While this plant is more suitable for the rock garden, it can be useful when planted for ground cover.

## Lamium

**Lamium galeobdolon 'Silver Carpet'** This is a

Fig 56 Buxus *(box) used as a border edging to a pathway with contrasting leaf colour of* Helichrysum angustifolium.

*Fig 57  The white flowered form of* Lamium maculatum, *a good carpeter.*

particularly fine form of deadnettle which is non-invasive, unlike some of its near relations. The nettled green and silver leaves and sprays of yellow flowers are most attractive.

**L.g. 'Taff's Little Angel'**  This is indeed well named when compared with the encroaching runners of the common yellow archangel. The leaves are smaller and silver patterned and the yellow flowers are almost as large as the species. I introduced this to commerce some years ago after one of my visits to North America where I had been in the company of a plantswoman who found this refined form as a sport, growing at the edge of woodland.

**Lamium maculatum 'Beacon Silver'**  This dead

nettle has outstanding silvery white foliage and rich pale pink flowers. This makes excellent ground cover for a shaded position.

**L.m. 'Chequers'**  This is a similar fine form but with deeper pink flowers than the above.

**Lamium maculatum 'White Nancy'**  An evergreen deadnettle with intensely white foliage and white flowers which will grow equally well in full sun or partial shade. This plant was named as a white flowered form of 'Beacon Silver' by an enthusiastic amateur gardener, who could see from his garden a monument and folly, known locally as 'White Nancy'. This famous folly near Bollington, Cheshire, is on the top of Kerridge Hill. It is in the shape of a small, domed sugarloaf, topped with a small ball. Frequently whitewashed, it is always an eye catcher.

**Lavandula lanata**  This species of lavender has heavily felted, silver-grey leaves and deep purple flowers, held on long stems. This plant forms a compact hummock. *Lavandula* 'Nana Alba' is a dwarf lavender with fine grey leaves that has short-stemmed white flowers in mid-summer.

**Leucanthemum hosmariense**  The finely divided, grey-green foliage is hummock forming and topped with large white ox-eye daisies during most months of the year. This plant is now known to botanists as *Chrysanthemopsis hosmariense* under which name it may already be found in nurseries.

**Leontopodium alpinum**  This is an edelweiss, a lovely, grey-leaved plant which has rather unusual felted white flowers. It would be more at home if planted in the rock garden.

**Marrubium cyllenum**  A plant that is seldom seen. It has beautiful, silky, apple-green leaves that have a white reverse and silver margin. This plant will tolerate a certain amount of shade.

**Mertensia asiatica**  A glaucous-leaved evergreen with trailing stems and pale blue flowers in late summer. This grows at its best in a cooler position on neutral to acid soil.

**Nepeta mussinii**  This is the common catmint with light-grey foliage and sprays of mauve-blue flowers. This should be pruned hard immediately after flowering.

**Origanum laevigatum**  A marjoram that has proved to be quite hardy in English gardens. The fine glaucous leaves on upright stems will bear sprays of pink-purple, hop-like flowers.

**O. rotundifolium** is a smaller species that has short stems with rounded blue-green leaves. The pale pink flowers arise from hop-like bracts.

**Pimelea prostrata**  A small shrublet forming absolutely prostrate mats of trailing stems. The closely packed, silvery glaucous leaves are studded in mid-summer with small white flowers, followed in early autumn with translucent white berries. A borderline hardy plant and ideal for the edge of a border, providing that the soil is well drained. It is more usually grown in scree beds or rock gardens.

**Potentilla argryophylla**  This plant makes neat clumps of silvery, strawberry-like foliage and in mid-summer, develops long sprays of yellow flowers.

**P. 'Nana Argentea'** (*P.* 'Beesii')  A small, shrubby plant with silky, silvery leaves and golden-yellow flowers.

**Ptilotrichum spinosum**  A small, spiny shrub that makes a dome-shaped grey mound that is studded in mid-summer with small, white flowers.

**P.s. roseum**  This is the same shrub but has flowers of a warm pink colour.

**Ruta chalepensis**  This is a member of the rue family and makes a mat of glaucous trailing stems covered, in summer, with yellow-green flowers. The handling of this plant can cause a rash on delicate skin.

**Salix helvetica**  A small, bushy shrub, whose young growth is hairy. The small grey-green leaves are white beneath. It can make a good hummock of ground cover.

**S. repens argentea**  This is a form of creeping willow with silvery, silky leaves and attractive catkins.

**Salvia multicaulis**  A prostrate plant with grey, rounded leaves and pink stems on the young growth. The upright purple-blue flowers drop to leave attractive bracts. This is borderline hardy in the North of England.

Fig 58   *A Chelsea scene, showing excellent blending of form and texture and good use of ground covering plants, particularly in the back border, with the grey leaves of* Santolina chamaecyparissus *in the foreground.*

**Santolina chamaecyparissus nana**   A smaller version of the cotton lavender, it has tight, slightly curled, evergreen foliage which is very aromatic.

**S.cham. nana 'Weston'**   A really dwarf version with white woolly foliage which does need to be planted in a well-drained site.

## Sedum

**Sedum cauticolum**   An attractive plant with trailing grey-purple leaves. In September it is covered by a mass of bright-pink flowers. A very good plant for the front of a small border.

**S. spathulifolium**   This plant forms low-growing mats of fleshy grey leaves with a purple tinge turning to plum-red in winter. The small yellow flower spikes appear in mid-summer.

**S.s. 'Cape Blanco'**   This has the same growth habit but the leaves are a very silvery white. It may be found under the incorrect spelling as 'Cappa Blanca'.

## Senecio

**Senecio cineraria**   The species plant is not totally hardy, however, the following forms are quite hardy in the south in all but the worst of winters.

**S.c. 'Ramparts'**   This forms a low mound of white, uncut leaves.

**S.c. 'White Diamond'**   A low-growing plant with a diamond-shaped leaf.

**Stachys byzantina** (lamb's lugs)   This is a well known cottage garden plant, often used for

*Fig 59 An excellent combination in leaf and colour of* Santolina *and* Phormium – *the New Zealand flax.*

edging beds and borders. The woolly leaves and heavily felted stems produce whorls of pink flowers in the summer. However, the leaves can become rather untidy when the flower spikes have developed. Hard cutting back immediately after flowering will rejuvenate the plant.

**S. byzantina 'Silver Carpet'** This is a non-flowering form whose foliage thus tends to remain in better condition throughout the summer months.

## Tanacetum

**Tanacetum densum amani** An attractive, low-growing, evergreen plant for full sun and reasonable drainage. It produces flat mats of finely divided, feathery foliage from which occasionally arise bright yellowy-gold tufted flowers in early summer.

**T. herderi** This plant makes bold mounds of finely cut grey leaves which will have silver stemmed, daisy-like gold flowers in early June.

**T. praeteritum**   This is a small shrub with twiggy stems and flat, filigree, fan-shaped, lead-grey leaves. Ox-eye daisy type flowers appear in June.

## Thymus

There are many thymes from which to choose and most have grey-looking leaves. However, some of the variegated varieties such as *T.* 'Silver Queen' with cream and green leaves, have an attractive, bright, silver appearance.

**Veronica spicata incana**   This plant forms prostrate mats of soft, broad, grey leaves and in midsummer, there are upright spikes of intense blue speedwell flowers.

Grey and silver foliage plants were the life-long interest of the late Mrs Desmond Underwood. She gathered together many such plants and grew them extremely well in her nursery, proving to all who saw her displays at horticultural shows that providing these plants have the right growing conditions, they are very rewarding. Unfortunately, her nursery is now closed. Readers will now need to hunt carefully in specialist nurseries and garden centres in order to build up a collection of grey and silver plants. No one establishment is likely to carry all the plants that are listed above.

## Plants for Shadier Positions

The following plants extracted from the lists above will look reasonable in partial shade:

*Acaena*
*Artemisia*

Fig 60   Galactites tomentosa, *a biennial thistle with extremely spiny but attractive leaves.*

*Dicentra*
*Lamium*
*Marrubium*
*Santolina*
*Senecio*

If you would like a grey or silver plant to grow in shade where the soil is not too dry but contains plenty of humus, I would recommend the Japanese painted fern, *Athyrium goeringianum* 'Pictum', which now has had a name change to *A. niponicum* 'Pictum'. This is a low-growing, slow-spreading fern whose fronds grow to about 9in (23cm) long with a width across the fronds of 4in (10cm). The fronds are silver-grey, flushed with pink at the centre. The effect of a large patch of this fern is silvery, but really, one needs to stand very close to study the fine pencilling of colour. This most attractive and unusual plant is probably the only coloured-leaf fern that is hardy outdoors in Britain.

I would also add that there are several heathers with outstandingly silvery leaves. One is 'Silver Knight' and another is 'Silver Queen'. The grey or silvery *callunas* are 'Silver Rose' and 'Silver Anne'; the latter has woolly grey foliage to 4in(10cm) high. Whilst the *callunas* are happiest in full sun, they need an acid soil.

## LAWNS

There is no finer example of ground cover than the lawn. Most gardens need a lawn to set off the other features such as shrub and herbaceous borders. The grass acts as a link, connecting the beds and borders together in the garden. A lawn allows frequent access to various parts of the garden and is a most effective green covering, wearing away only with excessive use. The aroma in the air given off by newly mown grass conjures up, for many people, images of a delightful summer's day.

Spreading plants in the foreground of a border, spilling over on to path edges, have a softening effect upon the straight lines of paths and lawn edges. Many people very effectively plant creeping rock plants or low-growing alpines into the cracks and crevices of pathways, on and around which there is no difficulty in walking. Particularly effective for such a planting are the many hundreds of species of carpeting alpines, many of which produce a glorious scent when walked on. In large gardens, a layout encompassing rough-mown grass between larger areas of garden, with a narrower, close-mown walkway, represents gardening at its best.

On the other hand, gardens of homes where children have grown up and there are no longer noisy, frolicksome games being played on the lawn, offer the opportunity for the plantsman and avid plant collector to cut out irregularly shaped beds to house an ever-increasing range of plants.

Walkways through lawns can be made using paving slabs of regular or irregular shapes, which can be sunk just below the surface of the mown lawn. These can look most attractive and do encourage the same pathways always to be used. They are particularly good in inclement weather, keeping feet away from the squelching turf. In effect, they are stepping-stones. Round concrete slabs are available in garden centres, in various colours and textures, very suitable for this purpose and economically priced. Also available are slightly more expensive simulated slices of tree trunks. They are irregularly shaped, the outer edges are dark resembling the bark and the inner surface is of a yellow colour simulating the inner soft wood of trees. These are well produced and are presumably made from rubber moulds of actual slices of tree trunks. They faithfully reproduce the somewhat raised, annular marks, or rings which produce a textured, non-slip surface. Once they have been laid and weathered for a season, they look very realistic and not at all like a man-made product.

Some garden centres stock a similar product in various sizes, made by a company in Warwickshire. These look like logs, made in the form of stepping stones, and have an old, weathered appearance. They are totally realistic

Fig 61   *The curved lawn, with the nearby pink and grey planting, enhances and encourages further exploration.*

in appearance and retain the fine moulding of the annular rings, incorporating the effect of logs that have shrunk and cracked in the process of weathering.

## Making a New Lawn

For a new lawn, you can select to start the lawn from seed or from turf. There are advantages and disadvantages with each method: seed is slow but less expensive than turf; standard quality turf will establish a lawn more quickly but

coarse grasses and a high percentage of rye grass often predominate and there is the likelihood of weeds being present. High quality, specially produced seeded turf is available in several weedfree grades. These turves are longer in length than standard turves and are easy to lay.

### Preparing the Site

To prepare the site for either seed or turf, take time to do it properly to avoid any long-term problems which could be troublesome for years.

*Fig 63   Stepping stones in a lawn, providing a firm, dry footing.*

Dig out any tree stumps, brick and other builder's debris, remove any large stones and perennial weed roots that you may find. The incorporation of sand or peat, depending upon your soil type, will be useful at this stage. Try to obtain a perfectly level surface without humps or hollows, so that once the lawn is established, there is a level surface for easy mowing.

## A Seed-Sown Lawn

It is good practice to leave the prepared site for a few months to settle before sowing grass seed. During this waiting time, weed seeds that germinate can be dealt with by using a basic weed-killer. Feed the soil with a fertilizer that is low in nitrogen but high in nitrates and potash.

Having ensured that the area is raked and level in readiness for sowing the grass seed, and having selected the right type of grass seed for the lawn that you wish to create, divide this area into strips 1 foot (30cm) wide by using garden canes as a guide line or by string, drawn tautly between two pegs. Scatter the seed evenly at the rate of 1 oz. per square yard (28g per square metre) and gently rake in. To prevent animals from disturbing the seed bed, stretch black thread across the site a couple of inches from the surface. To encourage good germination, moisten the soil with a fine spray from a hose or watering can that is fitted with a rose.

*Fig 62 (opposite)   Paving stones in the lawn lead to a focal point.*

83

## A Turf-Laid Lawn

Having carried out the ground preparation, order the best grade of turf that you can afford and order this as and when you want it. If your funds are limited, standard quality meadow turf will produce a durable lawn but will probably need attention to control the weeds that are bound to be present. Cultivated high quality seeded turf is grown from the best seed mixtures and is weed free. As this turf is specially grown from fine grasses such as bents and fescues, the price is considerably higher than for meadow or standard turves.

Do remember that a good quality lawn made from these turves needs more attention than one grown with the coarser grasses of the meadow turves. The worst weeds in a lawn are other grasses such as cocksfoot, couch and Yorkshire fog. They can take over the lawn and be very difficult to eradicate.

When the turf is delivered, try to carry out the laying within twenty-four hours of receipt, or open out each roll and water thoroughly. Do not leave the turves stacked for more than a day or two or they will start to go yellow and rot. Above all, do not forget that grass is a living plant, treat it well and you will be rewarded with a fine looking lawn. Providing that the ground is not frozen or under water, the best time to lay turf is between October and February. Laying turf at other times of the year, for instance, during hot, dry spells, will make it necessary to water the new turf to prevent it from drying out.

### Laying the Turf

Start with a straight row of turves, pressing the

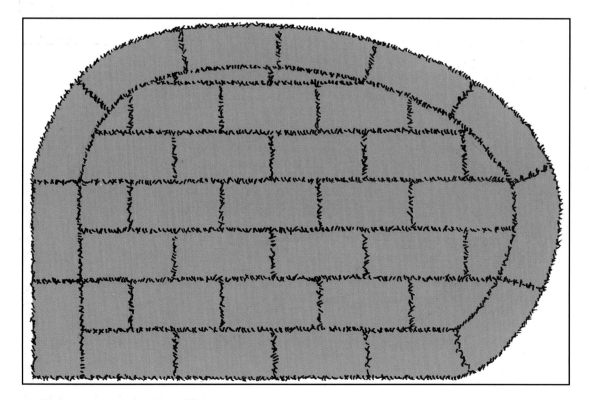

Fig 64  When laying shaped lawns, first lay whole turves around the edge so that smaller, irregularly shaped pieces finish away from the edge.

*Fig 65  Lawns – Mowing. Lawns need mowing once or twice a week in summer, depending on the weather; if it is very dry, once a week will be sufficient.*

ends together. Lay a plank on the turf and work from it to lay each subsequent row, staggering the joints from row to row, trimming off any excess with a sharp kitchen knife or edging iron. If you have a shaped lawn, start by laying the turves around the perimeter, any small, odd shaped sections will then finish away from the edge.

Immediately after laying, soak the turf thoroughly so that the water penetrates down to the underlying soil. Keep the turf moist until fully rooted.

If the turf is allowed to dry out after laying, it will shrink and these cracks will need to be filled in with soil. This chore can be avoided providing that the turf is regularly watered once or twice a week during warm, dry weather.

## Lawn Care

### Mowing

To many, mowing the lawn is a chore, sometimes carried out at irregular intervals, and often when the grass is far too long and looks terrible. It may be cut then, if only for appearances sake, when in fact, grass that has been allowed to grow tall has almost invariably allowed dominant grasses to take hold. In consequence, damage has possibly been done and you will no longer have a lawn, but tuffets of irregular shapes and gone will be the level, velvety green that is desired.

Mowing at frequent intervals and at specific heights will achieve an aesthetically pleasing surface. The grass mower, whether it be the hover-type or the cylinder mower, should be used from late spring to early autumn every five days. The

85

| MOWING REGIME | |
| --- | --- |
| **Month** | **Frequency** |
| January | None |
| February | None |
| March | Topping if mild |
| April | Once a week |
| May | Twice a week |
| June | Twice a week |
| July | Twice a week |
| August | Twice a week |
| September | Once a week |
| October | Topping if mild |
| November | Topping if mild |
| December | None |

every seven days. With the first cut of the season, the recommended heights above should be increased by ½in (1cm). Fine-leaved grasses, that give the quality ornamental lawn, will thrive and multiply when regularly cut. The regular cutting will discourage the establishment of coarser grasses.

In periods of drought, it is good policy not to mow the grass too closely but to leave up to 1in (2.5cm) of growth or a little more. Extremely short cut lawns do tend to dry out more quickly and brown more easily in these conditions.

## Collecting Grass Cuttings

On small, ornamental lawns, it is advisable to collect and compost the lawn mowings. In dry summers, these cuttings act as a mulch and reduce evaporation when placed around plants. If left on the lawn, the cuttings tend to get trodden into the house. On the other hand, if the cuttings are left on the lawn, these will decay and nutrients will be returned to the soil and this will have a

height of cut should be ½in (1cm), that is, leaving ½in (1cm) of grass coming up from the soil.

For a first-class ornamental lawn, cut every 2–3 days with the mower set to leave a growth of ¼–½in (0.5–1.0cm). Where there is a lawn that has to survive the activities of children, the grass can be left with 1in (2.5cm) of growth and cut

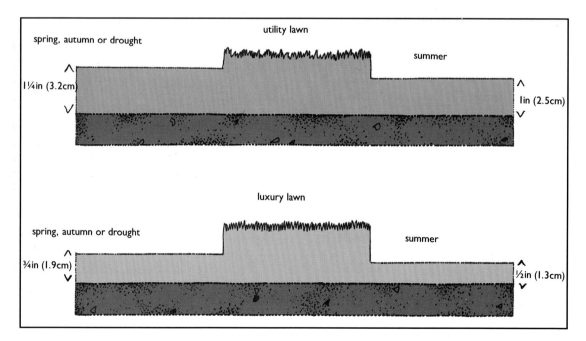

Fig 66 Levels of cut for utility and luxury lawns.

beneficial effect. If the cuttings are collected, this will avoid the re-growth of weed seeds and will also help to avoid the danger of building up lawn disease and creating a matting thatch of lawn detritus.

Mowers without grass boxes are lighter to operate and somewhat cheaper to buy. There are two basic designs of mowers, one of which is the hover mower that rides on a cushion of air. The less expensive types do not have a box or bag in which to gather the mowings. Such mowers have the advantage of enabling the sweeping of the lawn from left to right with the mowing action, whereas the cylinder mower produces the much sought after 'striped' finish. This latter is the type most commonly chosen and will be fitted with

a grass box for use on the ornamental, close-mown lawn.

## The Process of Mowing

To minimize work and to avoid the difficulties of turning mowers in confined spaces, cut the outer edge of the lawn first, making the strip wide enough to allow subsequent mowings to be carried out in straight parallel lines, turning the mower on to the already cut surface.

## Lawn Edging

Clearly defined lawn edges create an atmosphere of neatness and gives sharper lines of

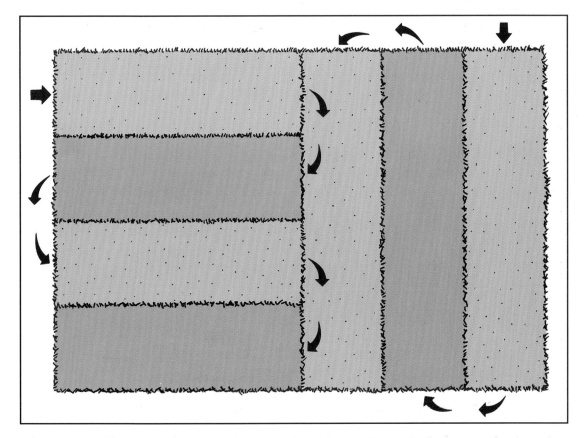

Fig 67   Changing the direction of the cut will ensure an even surface and will keep coarse grasses under control.

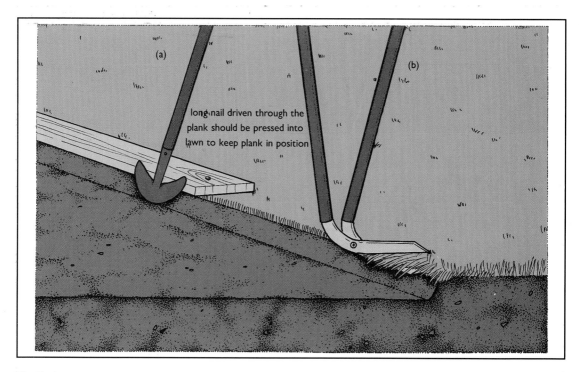

long nail driven through the
plank should be pressed into
lawn to keep plank in position

(a)
(b)

Fig 68   Lawns – edging. Neat edges set off a newly mown lawn perfectly: (a) a half-moon edging iron can be used on neglected or damaged edges; (b) on other lawns a pair of sharp edging shears will do the job well.

Fig 69   Edging .

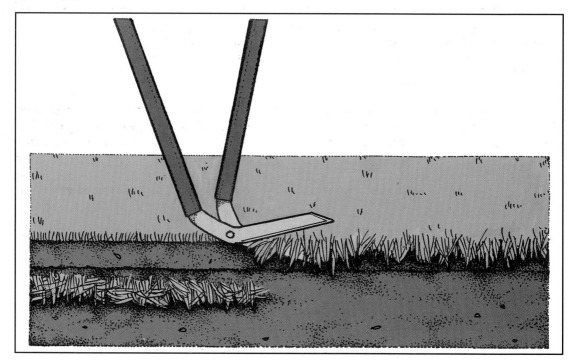

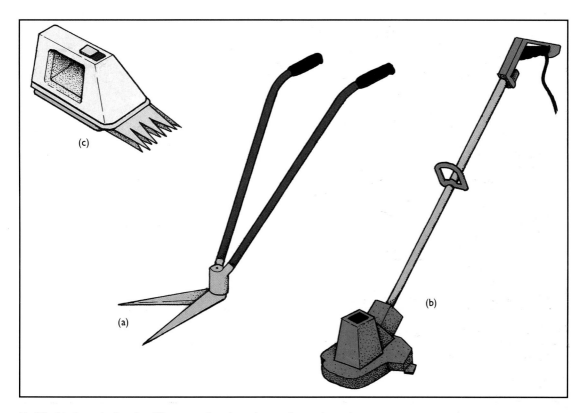

Fig 70 Horizontal trimming. There may be places in your lawn where the mower cannot reach – under spreading shrubs and around the base of trees, along fences and walls. You will need a horizontal trimmer such as (a) long-handled lawn shears; (b) a nylon cord trimmer or (c) a cordless trimmer.

demarcation. Use a sharp spade or half round edging iron. Trimming lawn edges should be an annual spring operation. Inevitably, the constant removal of turf over the years will result in the beds becoming larger and the lawn smaller. When this depletion has reached such proportions that you are encouraged to do something about the situation, remove a further 9in (23cm) wide strip of turf alongside the lawn edges and cut these into, say, 18in (46cm) pieces. Place these into the level border where you wish the new lawn edge to be. Fill the gap between the lawn and the turves with soil and sow with grass seed.

There are many types of permanent artificial edgings to lawns and these do reduce maintenance work. Treated planks of timber 2in (5cm)

thick can be placed along the lawn edge and held in position with wooden pegs or a long nail. This is inexpensive and easy to install. Plastic, aluminium and galvanized edging strips are very useful where curved edges to lawns are involved. These edging strips can be obtained from garden centres and have a useful life and place in the garden. As these types of lawn edgings can vary in size from 4–9in (10–23cm) in depth, they can affect lawn drainage by restricting water soak-away at the lawn edges. Artificial or natural stone bricks or concrete curves all make excellent lawn edges.

To prevent damage to mower blades, the top surface of the edging must be placed just below the lawn level and all types are best laid on a concrete base.

*Fig 71 Neat, well-trimmed lawn edges with ample space left for lawn shears to be used.*

## Trimming Lawn Edges

Frequent trimming is essential for a neat appearance as grass will inevitably creep over the edgings. Long handled edging shears are the most popular and give good results when they are sharp. Short handled shears of the type used for trimming hedges can be pressed into service; however, their use will tax your back when bending down to use them. There are battery operated shears, though these need regular re-charging of their inbuilt nickel cadmium batteries.

For the larger lawns, the investment of a mains electric nylon trimmer is worth considering, particularly those designed with a rotating swivel head which permits the cutting of lawn edges.

## Watering the Lawn

It is said that each square yard of lawn will lose four gallons of moisture each week during a hot, dry summer. While Britain normally receives adequate rain to keep lawns green and healthy, there are occasions when a lawn sprinkler may need to be used, particularly in hot, dry summers. It is as well to remember that when using a hose fitted with a sprinkler, that the water authorities require extra payment for any use of

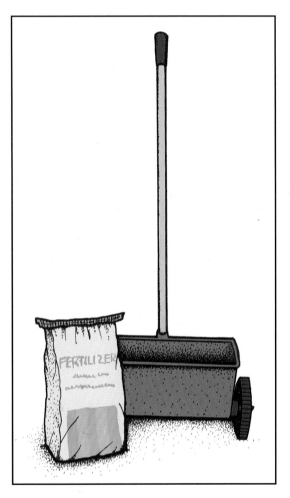

*Fig 72 Granular fertilizers can be applied by hand, or you can hire a wheeled applicator from your garden centre when making the purchase.*

90

a hose that is not hand held. Remember too, that if you water the lawn too often, you may be weakening its growth, as frequent, shallow watering encourages the roots of the grass to seek the surface. Even in the hottest weather, do not water more than twice a week. Choose a cool time of day to water, there is then the likelihood of there being more pressure in the mains early in the morning rather than in the evening when most people will be watering their gardens after returning home from work. In summers such as we have had in recent years, lawns have suffered, but grass roots have a great capacity to send up new shoots. The average cricket pitch, after a full season of fixtures, can resemble old coconut matting, but after some good rain it will fully recover.

## Weed Control

Unfortunately, many of the lawn weeds, in particular the clover, plantain and dandelion families, will have thrived at the expense of the grass. However, once the grass is growing strongly in the next spring, encouraged by a spring lawn feed, a concentrated effort should be made to dig out these weeds or use a lawn weed-killer. After this, a close mowing will improve the grass growth. Rake or scarify the surface and feed with a high phosphate and potash lawn fertilizer during the autumn. It is advisable to read the small print to ensure that you buy the right mixture for that particular season's use.

Several manufacturers have packaged a 'lawn care system' which feeds the grass and fights weeds and moss in one or more applications. Lawn weed-killers are available which are excellent for weed control on established lawns and these, when applied by a watering can fitted with a rose or sprinkle bar, are most effective and do not harm the grass. The selective herbicides in these lawn weed-killers kill broad-leaved weeds and their use on the lawn is best carried out when the weeds are actively growing. Soon after the treatment, you will notice that the leaves of the weeds become distorted. You can then be assured that the weed-killer will penetrate the plant down to its roots, causing the weed to die completely.

## Moss Control

Where your lawn is suffering from excessive moss growth — almost invariably caused by waterlogged subsoil — this unwanted growth can be controlled and killed by the use of a proprietary brand of moss killer. This product is usually applied with a watering can fitted with a rose or sprinkle bar. Moss killers usually show dramatic results as they are quick acting, turning the moss brown in a very few days. Rake out (scarify) the dead moss a week after treatment with the moss killer.

Whilst these packaged products help to prevent regrowth of the moss, the proud owner of a lawn should spend some time aerating these

Fig 73   A complete lawncare system will feed, weed and fight moss in one application.

areas by pricking the surface of the lawn every few inches with a garden fork to a depth of about 2in (5cm). Similarly, should you have bare patches on the lawn, often brought about by the killing off of excessive weed growth or by hard use in children's games which are always played on the same areas, rake or scarify them to form a fine seed bed. Scatter fine grass seed evenly at 1oz per square yard (28g per square metre). Mixing the grass seed with peat helps to provide an even spread. Spread a little extra moist peat or sifted garden soil to cover the area. Consolidate by patting down this area with the back of a spade and keep well watered. Strands of black thread stretched over the re-seeded area will help to keep animals and birds off until the grass is established.

## GENERAL OBSERVATIONS

My objective in writing this book has been to recommend plants that stay close to the ground to create a thick, low-maintenance covering, which, by its growth habit, prevents light reaching the soil beneath, where weed seeds would normally germinate. These plants are mainly hardy, durable, quick growing evergreens, providing dense leaf and stem cover; clump forming plants and stem rooting colonizers, both deciduous and evergreen. This listing does not include plants that have been described in other chapters.

It must be appreciated that the expressions 'fast growing' and 'drought tolerant' are relative terms, in that soil and site conditions can vary. Some soils may be moisture retentive, others dust dry at all times of the year, having no humus

*Fig 74* Euonymus fortunei *'Emerald 'n' Gold' making an excellent border edging.*

Fig 75   Salvia officinalis 'Tricolor'. The colouring of the felted leaves are most eye catching and the plant makes an excellent weed suppressor.

or substance to retain moisture below the first few inches (cms) of soil.

One of the enjoyable aspects of gardening is trying to confound statements that have been expounded about the hardiness of certain plants. This, of course, is a relative situation, as it is accepted that climatic conditions vary with latitude and altitude and are subject to local variations. Such statements about hardiness are usually based upon very small examples of experience, and some gardens can provide a sheltered area with its own microclimate for a suspect hardy plant to achieve success. However, ignoring plant hardiness advice will always be a gamble of course, and should not be attempted if an unsuccessful planting is likely to spoil the effect that you had hoped to achieve.

By no means can this listing be complete, as nature and the nurserymen are forever producing new varieties and cultivars which might well, tomorrow, be excellent plants for ground cover. Generally speaking, ground cover seldom takes centre stage in the garden, more often, it provides the backdrop for other plants to complete a garden landscape. Such ground cover planting creates interest in an often neglected area, the earth's floor, and these plants add texture and colour.

Ground cover can be of any height and coloured foliage lasts longer than most flowers and can have much the same impact. In a rather shady garden, one can appreciate the splashes of colour from variegated foliage which is shown to the best advantage when grown against dark backgrounds or neighbouring plants.

Flower beds, with large, established plantings

*Fig 76    The striking foliage of* Pulmonaria.

which join up to make a solid bank of foliage and flower, give little trouble. It is in places where bare soil surrounds shrubs or new plantings that weeds proliferate and need constant attention. A thick cover of vegetation conserves moisture and plants seem to do better when growing close to their neighbours rather than in isolation.

I know of no disadvantages connected with ground cover plants if they are chosen with care. They are inexpensive to buy compared with the purchase of an already well-grown shrub. They can be slow or quick to increase according to variety, easy to plant and can be kept in robust health by natural means without the use of chemical weed-killers, apart from their initial use for clearing the ground prior to planting. Such plants go a long way to providing natural beauty without the trouble of continual digging, hoeing and weeding.

You may be offered surplus ground cover plants from friends' gardens. Accept the clump-forming plants, but avoid at all costs any plants that increase by underground runners. If you have a limited budget with which to purchase plants, do consider propagation – this will increase your own stock and give you a surplus which can be exchanged with other gardeners, with the resulting increase in your selection and variety of plants.

## Nomenclature

In order to understand the plant names, it would be helpful to have a working knowledge of botanical nomenclature.

94

## Genus

This is the first word of a plant's name and refers to a group of plants that are similar in many botanical characteristics. Several related genera make up a family. A genus in turn contains a number of species.

## Species

This is the second word of a plant's name. A species is defined as a plant with characteristics that distinguish it from other plants of the same genus and are consistent from generation to generation.

## Variety

This is the third word in a plant's name. Varieties are distinctly different forms from the species. Where these have occurred naturally in the wild a varietal name is added and is also written in Latin and italicized.

## Cultivar

These are the many plants that arise through and are maintained in cultivation because of specific characteristics which are desirable. Usually, these plants have to be propagated vegetatively. The cultivar name is not written in italics but takes a capital letter and is enclosed between single quotation marks.

I hope that I may have persuaded some gardeners who think mainly in terms of flowers, that beauty and interest lie in other parts of plants as well, and that form and outline contribute much to the overall garden picture. Plants chosen with the same care as that used in the furnishing of your home can enhance the landscape and complement the architecture of the house.

*Fig 77  Hosta displaying excellent glaucous leaf colour and texture.*

## FURTHER SELECTED AND RECOMMENDED PLANTS

**Achillea**  Clump forming, carpeting, sun-loving plants requiring well-drained soil. Evergreen. Recommended are: *A. chrysocoma*; *A.* × 'kellereri'; *A. tomentosa*.

**Aegopodium** (variegated ground elder)

*A. podagraria* 'Variegatum'  Less vigorous than the common garden weed, it is fully hardy and is ideal for sun or shade. The leaves are broadly margined creamy white and die down in the winter to reappear in the spring. Best planted between barriers or contained within a bottom-less bucket.

**Ajuga** (bugle) An evergreen, carpeting, fast-growing plant, easy to cultivate. For sun or partial shade and a moist rather than a dry soil. All the following have blue flower spikes.

*A. reptans* 'Atropurpurea' Beetroot-coloured, shiny leaves.

*A.r.* 'Braunherz' A particularly dark brown-leaved form.

*A.r.* 'Burgundy Red' This variety has purple-red leaves.

*A.r.* 'Multicolor' This is sometimes offered as 'Rainbow' or 'Tricolor'. Leaves are brown with splashes of red and orange.

*A.r.* 'Variegata' The variegated leaves have a creamy white margin. Grows best in more moist soils.

**Alyssum** Prefers sun and well-drained soil. Ideal for slopes and fronts of borders. An ideal carpeter with grey leaves.

*A. saxatile* An evergreen, with masses of yellow flowers.

*A.s.* 'Citrinum' The flowers of this are a pale sulphur yellow.

## Arabis

*A. albida* Clump forming, evergreen, preferring a sunny spot with well-drained soil. Leaves are grey-green. White flowers in the spring.

*A.a.* 'Flore Pleno' This form has double white flowers.

*A.a.* 'Variegata' The leaves are edged creamy yellow.

**Armeria** (thrift) For sunny places, border verges or for planting between rocks to prevent annual weed growth. Prefers a well-drained, light soil.

*A. maritima* Dark green, grass-like leaves, pink flowers in early summer. A good carpeter.

There is a white-flowered form, *A.m.* 'Alba' and several named dark-red or rose-coloured flowered forms.

## Artemisia

*A. stelleriana* This plant prefers sun and well-drained soil. Downy leaves are grey-green. Evergreen and a sprawler, growing to only 1in (2.5cm) high.

**Asarum** (wild ginger) Plants for a cool, somewhat moister soil, excellent in shade. A good, evergreen spreader with rounded, dark-green glossy leaves. Flowers are most unusual and are hidden under the leaves in spring.

*A. europaeum* I grow this form which is often remarked upon for the freshness of its glossy, bright-green leaves.

*A. canadense* The leaves are larger than the above and have a coarse, hairy, matt appearance.

*A. shuttleworthii* This is a collector's item, having dull, hairy leaves marbled and patterned with silver.

There are forms from Japan with extremely contrasting silver marbling over the green, which, together with *A. hartwegii* and *A. shuttleworthii* are native to North America and are the subjects for plant collections. In a similar way there are people who collect the many different leaf markings of *Cyclamen hederifolium*. These fine marbled forms of *Asarum* will need to be sought from specialist nurseries.

**Aubrieta** For sun and soil that is well drained, for border edges and edges of rose beds and rock gardens. A carpeting plant, partially deciduous, flowering in the spring.

*A. deltoidea* There are many coloured flowered forms. Two forms with variegated margined leaves are *A.d.* 'Argenteo-Variegata' with silver

*Fig 78  A well-grown specimen of* Artemisia.

variegation and *A.d.* 'Aureo-variegata' with golden variegation.

**Berberis**  Berberis are easily grown, sun-loving, hummock-forming evergreen shrubs with prickly growth. Spring flowering.

*B. stenophylla* 'Prostrata' with horizontal, ground covering growth is sometimes offered as *B. darwinnii* 'Prostrata'.

**Bergenia**  Hardy perennials, excellent for shaded areas. Large, leathery leaves turn in the autumn with flushes of yellow and red. Handsome pink, white or rose flower spikes appear in the spring. They combine well with hostas and ferns.

Usually grown is *B. cordifolia* and *B. purpur-* *ascens*, this is sometimes listed as *B. delavayi*. There are many hybrids with variations of flower colour.

These plants are used extensively by landscape architects for they are economical to produce (established clumps split readily), and their leaves and flowers are extremely durable in inclement weather. However, I am forced to think of them as 'cabbages with elephant's ears' – but they do make good ground cover.

**Campanula** (bell flower)  These are sun loving and will grow in dappled shade, usually used in the rock garden or in borders. Wide blue, up-turned bell-like flowers.

*C. carpatica*  Deciduous and a little clump former 9in (23cm). There are many garden forms

97

*Fig 79*  Campanula portenschlagiana *flowering profusely.*

of *C. carpatica* with flower colours ranging from white to purple.

*C. latiloba*  This is a little taller than the previous form, and has many interesting garden hybrids with flower colours varying from white to violet-blue.

*C. portenschlagiana*  This is a deciduous, mid-summer flowering spreader with 8in (20cm) flowering stems and clustered lilac-blue bell flowers. This is sometimes listed as *C. muralis*.

*C. poscharskyana*  Evergreen, with trailing shoots and lavender-blue flowers. There are various colour forms from white, through pink to a bright blue, flowering in midsummer.

This, and the previous Campanula, are spreaders and make a very effective ground cover, but are best given areas where they can romp without smothering small, treasured plants.

**Carex**  These are sedges with lovely, strap-like leaves. Usually best grown in dappled shade, or at least in a moist soil. They are evergreen and clump forming in the main and because their leaves arch, they are effective weed suppressors.

*C. brunnea* 'Variegata'  This has a lovely white edge to the leaves.

*C. comans* 'Bronze Form'  Very narrow, bronze leaves and very architectural in its growth habit.

*C. conica* 'Hino-ken-sugi Variegata'  A Japanese narrow-leaved, clump former with a narrow, cream variegation.

*C. oshimensis* 'Evergold'  A most attractive

variegated plant with ¼in (0.5cm) wide leaves. Because of the arching of these leaves, it makes a superb, colourful mop, hugging the ground. It is sometimes listed as as *C. morrowii* 'Evergold'.

*C. elata* 'Aurea' (Bowles golden sedge) This plant has superb, rich gold leaves.

*C. riparia* 'Variegata'  A good cream margin to the leaves. Both this and the above *Carex* are 'travellers' and can pop up 6in (15cm) or so away from where they were planted, in moist soil. Perhaps best planted at the edge of a pond or in a wild, boggy area. Otherwise, contain them in a bottomless bucket.

## Cerastium

*C. tomentosum* (snow in summer)  An invasive plant but admirable when used where it cannot encroach into other plants and small shrubs for sun and well-drained soil. The plant makes dense mats of silvery grey leaves, is evergreen and white flowers appear in early summer. Best clipped to the ground in the autumn.

*C.t. columnae*  This is a unique form in that it is not so rampant, but has the same superb silver-grey leaves. This particular plant needs to be sought in specialist nurseries, usually those dealing in alpine plants.

## Convallaria (lily of the valley)  A deciduous spreader, taking time to settle down. It will thrive in sun or shade but needs ample moisture at its roots.

*C. majalis* 'Fortin's Giant'  This is the best form, having larger white bells with a delicious scent.

*C.m.* 'Rosea'  This is a pink flowered form.

*C.m.* 'Prolificans'  Most of the white flowers are more or less double.

*C.m.* 'Variegata'  The leaves are vertically striped with a narrow cream band.

*C.m.* 'Hardwick Hall'  This has larger leaves that have a creamy yellow margin. This is probably a different species from *C. majalis*.

## Cornus (dogwood)

*C. canadensis*  A native of Alaska, found in an area stretching to New Mexico and West Virginia. Always grown in a moist, acidic soil in open woodlands. It is a deciduous spreader, growing by non-invasive underground runners and growing no taller than 9in (23cm). The tiny flower clusters appear in early spring, surrounded by 4–6 white bracts. The oval leaves are 3in (8cm) in length and are a deep, rich green, turning to yellow-red in autumn. This *Cornus* makes an excellent ground cover around rhododendrons and such similar plants which also require acidic soil.

## Cotoneaster  There are many cotoneasters that are suitable for ground cover. They have attractive flowers in spring and berries in the autumn.

*C.* 'Skogholm'  A hybrid which is widely used by professional landscape gardeners as a form of trouble-free, quick-spreading ground cover.

*C. adpressus*  A deciduous shrub with minute leaves which makes an excellent hummock of about 12in (30cm) in height.

*C. congestus*  This makes an evergreen carpet growing only 4in (10cm) off the ground, with white flowers in the spring and red berries in the autumn.

*C. dammeri*  An evergreen carpeter, similar to the above.

*C. horizontalis*  Deciduous, with the leaves taking on good autumn tints. The small white flowers, followed later by red berries, are held on fern-like branches.

*C.h.* 'Variegatus'  Less vigorous than the green form but particularly attractive for its cream-edged leaves.

There are many other cotoneasters that can be obtained with varying growth habits.

## Cytisus (broom)  Most brooms make excellent

*Fig 80* Cotoneaster horizontalis *with* Alchemilla mollis *in flower.*

ground cover and although deciduous, make impenetrable hummocks or carpets of growth.

*C. × kewensis* An excellent hybrid with yellow pea-like flowers. Grows to only 10in (25cm) or so high but spreads several feet (about 1 metre) or more outwards.

**Dicentra** Very good for growing in sun or partial shade, these are best in good, light, moist woodland soil. Most have fresh green, ferny leaves and are deciduous. They are spreading plants and grow to 12in (30cms) or so in height. They flower in the spring. Named plants to look for are 'Adrian Bloom', 'Bacchanal' and 'Bountiful'.

*D. spectabilis* This is a tall grower in both the pink and white flowered forms but is ineffective as ground cover as the plants die down early in summer. However, they are most attractive used in the herbaceous border.

## Duchesnea

*D. indica* This forms a dense, low mat with strawberry-like leaves and yellow flowers. The plant spreads rapidly by runners that root at every node. An excellent ground cover plant but is undoubtedly very rampant. As it is surface rooting, it can be controlled easily by cutting back the far-reaching runners. Should it overreach into other plants, the runners can be easily pulled out.

*D.i.* 'Harlequin' is a form with variegated leaves and may possibly be found under the invalid name of *D.i.* 'Variegata'.

**Epimedium** (barrenwort) These grow well in sun or shade in good soil and spread with creeping roots to make a 9in (23cm) high ground covering. After planting, they take time to settle down and become established. The heart-shaped leaves are prettily tinted pink in spring and look very attractive. Remove the older leaves of the deciduous species in the winter to reveal the flowers that will appear in spring.

*E. × rubrum* A hybrid with crimson flowers.

*E. × versicolor* This has pale pink flowers.

*E. × warleyense* This is a species with orange-red and yellow flowers.

All three mentioned above are deciduous and can be propagated by splitting established clumps.

**Euonymus** Almost any of the *E. fortunei* clones make attractive ground cover. They are of a lax, trailing growth habit, evergreen and hummock forming.

*E.f.* 'Emerald Gaiety' and *E.f.* 'Emerald 'n' Gold' are widely available and very attractive with their variegated leaves.

**Ferns** (*see* pages 38–45)

**Festuca**   Ideal carpeting grass which can be obtained with many different leaf colourings.

*F. glauca*   Grows to only 6in(15cm) in height and has most attractive blue-grey narrow leaves.

There are named forms of *F. glauca* with leaves of a glaucous hue. These are *F.g.* 'Blue Fox' and *F.g.* 'Meerblau' (Blue Sea).

**Fragaria** (strawberry)   A carpeting plant, particularly the alpine strawberry, the fruits of which are delicious to eat.

*F.* 'Baron Solemacher'   This is clump forming and does not produce runners; good for partially shaded areas.

*F. vesca* 'Multiplex'   An attractive carpeter, rooting as it grows. Popularly known as 'Bowles's Double' having double flowers.

*F.v.* 'Plymouth Strawberry'   A close relative of the alpine strawberry. It is familiarly known as the 'All Green Strawberry' as all parts of its flowers and fruits are green. The fruits are not particularly palatable. In certain conditions, I have known the fruits to colour slightly to a greeny-pink. This garden 'oddity' has been maintained in cultivation since the days of Canon Ellacombe, a century ago.

*F.v.* 'Monophylla' also dates back as far as the above and is known as the one-leaved Strawberry.

**Gaultheria**   Essentially for lime free soils and best only for the warmer gardens.

*G. nummularioides*   Carpet rooting and evergreen with white or pink tinted flowers and blue-black berries.

*G. procumbens*   An evergreen spreader, the flowers are like tiny white bells and the fruits are scarlet.

Both the above mentioned grow only to a few inches (cms) high.

*Fig 81   Geraniums, making good ground cover with foliage and flower.*

**Geranium**   Almost all hardy herbaceous geraniums are assets to any garden and are happy in any soil except badly drained clays. They are indispensable as ground cover, having beauty of leaf and flower. There are considerably more than fifty different species and named hybrids from which to choose.

*G. renardii*   Clump forming and deciduous. Grey-green, velvety leaves, with white flowers that have narrow veins appearing in early summer.

*G. sanguineum*   There are several forms with differing flower colours:

*G.s. album* is white flowered; *G.s.* 'Glenluce' with pink flowers; *G.s. lancastrense* with pink and crimson veined flowers.

Fig 82   Geraniums can provide total ground coverage.

The last three mentioned are spreading plants and are deciduous. All can be readily divided from established clumps to increase your stock.

**Geum** (Avens)   Clump forming plants that grow well in moist soil, in sun or partial shade.

*G. × 'Borisii'* and *G. rivale*   Both have dark green, rounded leaves with good, vivid orange and coppery, yellowish-pink flowers respectively in early summer. There is also a white flowered form of *G. rivale*.

*G. 'Leonard's Variety'*   This is a particularly good form.

### Hakonechloa

*H. macra* 'Alboaurea'   This superb grass, introduced from Japan in recent years, makes an ex-cellent, arching, golden hummock, but can be very slow to spread outwards. To my mind, this is one of the best plants of recent introduction that should be in every garden and grown in full sun.

**Heathers**   *See* pages 30–34.

**Hebe**   Most of the *Hebes* that would be categorized as ground cover are hummock forming, evergreen shrubs. They are hardy in all but the coldest districts and all blend well with heathers. There are many to choose from.

*H.* 'Carl Teschner'   Recently re-named *H.* 'Youngii'   This makes a spreading hummock of about 9in (23cm) in height and has small, dark green leaves and violet-blue flowers.

*H. × franciscana* 'Blue Gem'   This is taller than the above with light blue-green leaves.

*H. pinguifolia* 'Pagei'   A dwarf form with white flowers and glaucous blue-grey foliage.

**Hedera**   *See* pages 45–57.

**Herbs**   *See* pages 57–62.

**Heuchera** (coral plant)   These plants are excellent clump formers for sun or partial shade. Almost all the garden hybrids make good clumps and if planted close together, knit into a carpet. The flowers are usually bell-shaped, coral pink or red and ½in (1cm) long, borne on 2in (5cm) flowering spikes from June until September. The leaves are usually almost evergreen which take on red tints in the winter. Species to look for are:

*H. americana*   This has leaves of a purplish-green.

*H. micrantha*   A plant with hairy leaves of a marbled greyish-green.

*H.m.* 'Palace Purple'   A particularly attractive plant, with shiny, deep purple leaves.

*H. sanguinea*   Dark green leaves and scarlet flowers.

*H.s.* 'Snow Storm' and *H.s.* 'Taff's Joy'   These two plants have differing attractive, variegated, white-splashed leaves. 'Snow Storm' was selected in America and *H.s.* 'Taff's Joy', the older of the two forms, was selected in England.

**Hosta** (plaintain lily)   *Hostas* are now very popular, enjoying a revival of interest. They are bred extensively in America and many good, named forms with attractive attributes, particularly those with variegated leaves, are to be found in almost every nursery and garden centre. There are ten or more species and a few hybrids.

*Hostas* enjoy growing in sun or partial shade but resent damage from drips if planted under trees. Excellent planted in north-facing borders or with shrubs; they need a good rich humus soil. Established clumps are easily split to provide extra plants. They are often chosen for their leaves which can be variously edged – from white, through cream to gold; some are glaucous blue and others a light or dark green. In almost all gardens, slugs can play havoc by eating and disfiguring the leaves. Slug traps and pellets are a 'must' to control them.

**Hypericum** (St. John's wort)   These can be found as herbaceous plants or as shrubs.

*H. calicynum*   A realistic source of ground cover, evergreen and a hummock former, large yellow flowers are borne in summer. A good drought survivor, but spreads freely by underground shoots and runners. In some gardens, the planting is regretted as it is so invasive.

*Fig 83   A bold planting of a variegated* Hosta *with the red flowers of* Nicotiana.

*Fig 84 A cool corner with* hostas *in variety.*

*H. rhodoppeum* An evergreen with a carpeting habit, growing to about 3in(8cm) in height. Grey, downy leaves and deep yellow flowers.

**Iberis** (candytufts)

*I. sempervirens* A plant of quite low stature, clump forming and sprawling. Usually used to tumble over edges of rock gardens and fronts of borders. Flat, white flower clusters appear in early spring at the top of stems with narrow, dark green leaves. These long stems bend to the ground and readily root. Best clipped back by a few inches (cms) after flowering, to keep the plant bushy.

Named forms to look for are:

*I.s.* 'Snowflake' and *I.s.* 'Little Gem'.

**Juniper** *See* pages 36–38.

**Lamium** (deadnettle) There are many species that are excellent plants to be grown in full sun or partial shade. Many have a rampant habit but can easily be removed should they grow out of their allotted space. They make very good ground cover when grown under large shrubs.

*L. galeobdolon* The attractive, heart-shaped leaves have a good splash of silver and few plants can equal its beauty and brilliance when planted under trees. Flowers are yellow and appear in early summer.

*L.g.* 'Silver Carpet' A clump forming plant.'

*L.g.* 'Herman's Pride' This is very similar to *L.g.* 'Silver Carpet' in its leaf colouring of silver but is possibly more compact in its growth.

*L. maculatum* There are attractive forms with differing flower colours:

*L.m.* 'Album'   A variety with white flowers.

*L.m.* 'Roseum'   A similar variety, but with clear pink flowers.

*L.m.* 'Aureum'   This is a form with yellow leaves.

There are other selected silver splashed leaf forms:

*L.m.* 'Chequers' and *L.m.* 'White Nancy' which is white flowered.

**Lavender**   *see* page 6l.

**Liriope**   These are evergreen, slow clump-formers or spreaders and require sun and well-drained soil.

*L. muscari*   With strap-like leaves up to 15in (30cm) with 8in (20cm) spikes of lavender flowers in the autumn. This is possibly the easiest to obtain.

*L. spicata*   This is lower growing with leaves of only 8in(20cm) and has white flower spikes in late summer. There are many other *Liriope* species and many have white or yellow variegated leaves. These plants are extensively used in parts of the U.S.A. as ground cover, and this genus, together with *Ophiopogon*, a near relative, are fashionable to almost cult proportions. Surprisingly, there are few nurseries and sources to obtain these highly desirable and attractive plants, either in this country or in the U.S.A.

**Lonicera** (honeysuckle)   Some gardening writers advocate pegging down forms of *Lonicera* as ground cover, in large, wild areas. However, from plantings that I have seen, they tend to produce an unwieldy mass of leaves and flower only on the topmost surface of the branch framework. Should there be a tree or shrub nearby, this quickly becomes engulfed.

**Lysimachia** (creeping Jenny)

*L. nummularia*   Excellent for partial shade, this grows particularly well if the soil is moist when the plant makes a dense carpet a few inches

high. It is carpet-rooting, evergreen, with small, bright green, rounded leaves set oppositely and bright yellow flowers. Easily propagated by splitting clumps or rooting tips.

*L.n.* 'Aurea'   The leaves of this variety are a golden yellow colour.

**Mazus**   This alpine plant grows satisfactorily in moist soil in sun or shade and is excellent for small-scale planting around walkways or as edgings. Forms a thick, low mat only 1–2in (2–5cm) high, rooting along its stem. The flowers are purplish-blue from late spring.

**Mentha**   *See* page 60.

**Milium**

*M. effusum* 'Aureum'   This is a grass, popularly known as 'Bowles's Golden Grass'. The leaves are 10in (25cm) or so high and the plant is deciduous and clump forming. Every garden should have this plant. It should be allowed to seed so that you have plenty of progeny to create a massed planting to make an effective ground cover. Because of its attractive golden colouring, it will lighten any dark or shady corner in the garden. Any unwanted stray seedlings are readily seen and removed with a slight stoop and a gentle pull close to the ground.

**Nepeta** (catmint)

*N. x faassenii*   An excellent evergreen clump former for sunny edges of borders or even under trees and shrubs. Flowers are lavender blue. Probably not a good plant for certain gardens in the northern parts as it resents extreme cold. May still possibly be offered for sale as *N. mussinii*.

**Ophiopogon**

*O. japonicus* and *O. intermedius*   Both are spreading plants with 9in (23cm) dark, shiny green, strap-like leaves and white flowers in summer and early autumn.

*O. planiscapus* 'Nigrescens' The 10in (25cm) long, slightly arching, strap-like leaves, I contend, are the blackest coloured leaves of any plant in our gardens. It makes very good ground cover if you can obtain sufficient for a massed planting. Purple flowers appear in late summer. Unfortunately, it is not a cheap plant but it comes tolerably true from seed and this is possibly the best way to bulk up for your massed planting.

### Pachysandra

*P. terminalis* An evergreen perennial, widely used as ground cover in shady locations. Spreads rapidly by underground runners to form a dense cover of essentially uniform height. Propagate by division or by rooting cuttings. This is an excellent plant for large-scale planting under trees or, on a smaller scale, under the shade of small evergreen shrubs. There is a variegated form: *P.t* 'Variegata'.

### Petasites

*P. fragrans* This is a rampant spreader in all soils, a vigorous colonizer with large, rounded and felted leaves and is deciduous. The small, 9in (23cm) flowering spikes appear in early spring. I have seen this plant recommended as ground cover, but would warn readers not to plant it in the garden as it is far too invasive. It is quite deeply rooted and even the smallest piece of white root will produce yet another lusty plant. It even seems to thrive on weed-killer!

Similar species are:

*P. hybridus* (butterbur) and *P. albus* These should not be planted, even though their leaves and flowers are attractive and most certainly do make good ground cover, almost totally suppressing weeds because of their overlapping leaves.

*P. japonicus* 'Variegatus' The extra large, rounded leaves to 2ft (0.60m) or more across, are irregularly splashed with a golden colour, a most effective plant for the wild garden. It is more or less surface-rooting and therefore easily removed if unwanted.

**Polygonum** (knotweed) For sun or shade, undoubtedly preferring a damp soil, but many will grow in the diverse soils to be found in our gardens.

*P. affine* A carpet-rooting plant, growing to 2ft (0.60m) in height, the narrow leaves are a bright green, turning red in winter before leaf fall. The pink, erect, flowering spikes are about 12in (30cms) tall.

Other colour flowered forms are:

*P.a.* 'Darjeeling Red'; *P.a.* 'Donald Lowndes' and *P.a.* 'Superbum'.

Other species with good carpeting qualities:

*P. amplexicaulis* and *P. bistorta*.

Two excellent clump formers are:

*P. virginiana* 'Variegata' and *P.v.* 'Painter's Palette' Both forms have attractive, elliptical, yellow- and green-splashed leaves, with 'Painter's Palette' also having a red 'V' shape on the leaves. This last form mentioned was first offered in commerce by the Plantsmen Nursery, unfortunately a nursery no longer in existence.

The polygonums mentioned above have been reclassified under the genus *Persicaria*.

**Polygonum cuspidatum** (or *P. reynoutria*) (Japanese knotweed) This is now considered to be so rampant that regulations now prohibit its planting in cultivated land, although there is an excellent variegated form:

*P.c.* 'Variegata' The leaves are yellow, green and red in irregular blotches and this is worthy of being grown in a very large tub to appreciate the colouring of the young growths.

*P. cuspidatum* and its older name *P. reynoutria* have been recently incorporated into the new genus *Fallopia*, and the variegated plant mentioned above is now more correctly labelled as *F. japonica* 'Variegata'.

**Rosa** *See* pages 62–70.

## Rubus

*R. tricolor*  This is perhaps the best *Rubus* for ground cover purposes; it is a most rapid carpeting grower, rooting as it goes, and can be grown in almost any soil in sun or shade. It has oval, toothed, glossy, dark green leaves and shiny stems that are covered in red-brown hairs. There are occasional, cup shaped, small white flowers and excellent, edible, raspberry-like fruits. I can only presume that its name – *tricolor* – refers to the green leaves, white flowers and red fruits.

*Rubus idaeus* 'Aureus'  With its typical bramble leaves, this plant looks most attractive in pots when offered for sale. However, in a very few years, the area in which it is planted becomes a thicket of growths, appearing at intervals of 6–9in (15–23cm). The runners travel underground, sending up growths of leaves at 6in (15cm) or so intervals. This, therefore, should be treated as a plant that is *not* really suitable for small garden culture.

**Sedum**  There are many clump forming *Sedums* that are excellent in the herbaceous border. However, the carpet forming *Sedums* are more correctly associated with attractive plants in the rock garden, such as *S. spathulifolium* and particularly, *S.s.* 'Purpureum', which has grey-purple succulent leaves.

## Stachys (lamb's ears)

*S. byzantina*  The best form and an excellent carpeter is *S.b.* 'Silver Carpet', a non-flowering form with grey-white woolly leaves. Very good ground cover for poor soils in full sun. There are excellent forms of the above:

*S.b.* 'Cotton Boll'  A plant with ball-like flowering spikes.

*S.b.* 'Primrose Heron'  The leaves of this plant are a yellow-grey.

*S.b.* 'Variegata'  A recently selected variegated form, as yet not given a clonal name. The leaves are splashed with white. In this form, it is necessary to prune out any uncharacteristic, non-variegated leaves.

*S. macrantha*  Another good carpeting plant with dark green, hairy leaves. Purple sage-like flowers in whorls appear in early summer.

## Teuchrium (wild germander)

*T. chamaedrys*  For sun and well-drained soil. It makes a 9in (23cm) clump, having small, dark green, hairy leaves and is deciduous. Soft pink flowering heads are held on 9in (23cm) spikes.

*T.c.* 'Variegatum'  The leaves are attractively golden splashed. Usually seen as a 'spot' plant in a rock garden. However, if a massed planting can be arranged, it makes very good ground cover.

*T. pyrenaicum*  An excellent carpeter growing some 2in (5cm) above the ground. Rounded hairy leaves, flowers are cream with purple marking.

*T. scorodonia*  This is clump forming, although its lax growth will often root where it touches the ground and so can make quite large clumps.

*T.s.* 'Crispum'  The leaf edges are attractively crimped on this variety.

*T.s.* 'Crispum Marginatum'  There are noticeably white crimped edges to the leaves of this plant which was selected by the late Eric Smith and put into commerce by the now defunct Plantsmen Nursery.

## Tiarella

*T. cordifolia* and *T. wherryi*  Excellent in almost all soils, in semi-woodland or beneath shrubs. Evergreen, clump-forming and carpeting, growing to 5in (13cm) high off the ground. The lobed, green, hairy leaves become bronze in winter, the flowering, feathery spikes are about 9in (23cm) in height.

**Vinca** (periwinkle)  For shade or partial shade, it is an effective ground cover, the growths rooting at almost every node, but taking some years to cover the soil. The flowers are attractive and

*Fig 85   Veronica prostrata* 'Trehane'. *The yellow leaves contrast well with the exquisite bright blue flower spikes.*

borne on shorter growths from the clump. Usually identified in the mind as having blue flowers, there are, however, several selected different coloured flower forms.

*V. major* 'Reticulata'  This has an interesting, reticulate leaf pattern, apparent only at certain times of the year.

*V.m.* 'Variegata'  The leaves are cream edged. This is sometimes offered as *V.m.* 'Elegantissima'.

*V.m.* 'Maculata'  The green leaves have a yellowish centre. Sometimes offered as *V.m.* 'Surrey Marble'

*V. minor*  This has many forms and particularly attractive is:

*V.m.* 'Alba Variegata'  The green leaves are edged with white.

*V.m.* 'Argenteovariegata'  This has similar leaves to the above.

*V.m.* 'Aureovariegata'  The leaves of this plant have a gold variegation.

There is a golden leaved form *V.m.* 'Aurea' and several double flowered forms.

## Waldsteinia

*W. ternata*  With dark-green, well lobed, smooth leaves and bright yellow, strawberry-like flowers. A carpeting plant, growing some 4in(10cm) from the ground, making ideal ground cover of thick mats which look attractive throughout the year. All growth root as it carpets the soil. It can be shy to flower in some gardens.

I hope that the plants mentioned above will provide an ample selection, albeit limited by the confines of the book.

# CHAPTER 7

# Terraces, Patios and Paths

Gardeners often forget to sit back and enjoy looking at the fruits of their labours. Garden designers realize the attraction of just sitting and looking. Through the pages of gardening magazines and in many recently published books, we are continually encouraged to lay paving slabs and make a patio, so much so that to be without a patio would seem to be unfashionable. It is also stressed that a patio makes a 'low maintenance garden'. And so it would, were we to lay out the whole garden in this manner.

The 'low maintenance garden' is a phrase that

*Fig 86   Wide, practical terrace steps with* Cordyline terminalis, *variegated* Iris *and* Heuchera *in the foreground.*

seems to be very popular with gardening writers. They consider it desirable for us to have exhibition gardens consisting of little else than paving slabs and other brick structures of walls and raised beds, which, in their parlance, is called 'hard landscaping'. 'Soft landscaping' refers to the plants, the flower borders and lawns, which we know simply as gardening.

Whatever we feel about these trends, patios and terraces can be considered as a form of ground cover, and within certain limitations, can be constructed to form a desirable feature in the garden, providing a relaxing, safe area for leisure. Families with young children, elderly gardeners and those with certain types of

disabilities will undoubtedly benefit from an area such as this.

The word patio comes from the Spanish word *patyo*. It has slipped into our vocabulary to described any flat sitting area in the garden. The Spanish build houses around an inner courtyard, open to the sky, to enable them to have a cool and shaded area in which to relax, away from the hot sun. In other countries people tend to use patios as clean, dry, uncluttered areas where they can enjoy the sun in our changeable and often inclement weather.

Today, there are many different types of hard surface materials to choose from, but whichever type is chosen, remember that these surfaces

*Fig 87 A quiet corner.*

can become slippery after a period of time. There are many good preparations that can be applied to remove any encrustations of green algae to ensure a safe and clean footing.

## SIMPLE GUIDELINES FOR CONSTRUCTION

A deep, firm, level base for the hard surface needs to be well constructed from the outset, otherwise the surface will soon become an uneven, puddled and weedy area, particularly between the intersections and joins of the paving slabs.

The type of base used will depend very much on the surface to be constructed and the condition of the ground upon which it is laid. On newly excavated land, it is essential to provide a deep, firm, level base with good drainage to avoid settlement problems later on. To ensure good drainage, all hard surfaces must be laid so that they slope almost imperceptibly towards an outer edge, and if for a terrace or patio, away from the house. If there is no natural soakaway such as a flower bed, then a drainage system should be provided.

Pavings and bricks look very attractive and it is essential to use a good, rich cement mixture to grout between the materials used, otherwise weeds will take a hold and cause the terrace or patio to become unsightly and labour intensive. Even when materials such as tarmacadam or concrete are used, it can be seen on occasions that even these almost impenetrable barriers are pierced by some of the strongest of perennial weeds. Weeds will find their way through cracks, or weed seeds will soon germinate and gain a foothold in the surface beneath the cracks.

Any such cracks will not only provide a site for weeds to grow but will allow water to enter, which in winter turns to ice which expands the cracks. This expansion and subsequent contraction, assisted by the growth of weeds, starts the disintegration of the hard surface.

It is usual to lay paving slabs and large pieces

Fig 88   The golden leaves of Viburnum opulus 'Aureum' effectively used with Genista pilosa as a path edging.

of crazy paving on a bed of level sand with a depth of at least 3in (8cm). However, on recently made-up land, a layer of hard core should be put down and compressed below the sand. (See Figs 90–91).

When laying crazy paving, which may be of varying thicknesses, great care should be taken

111

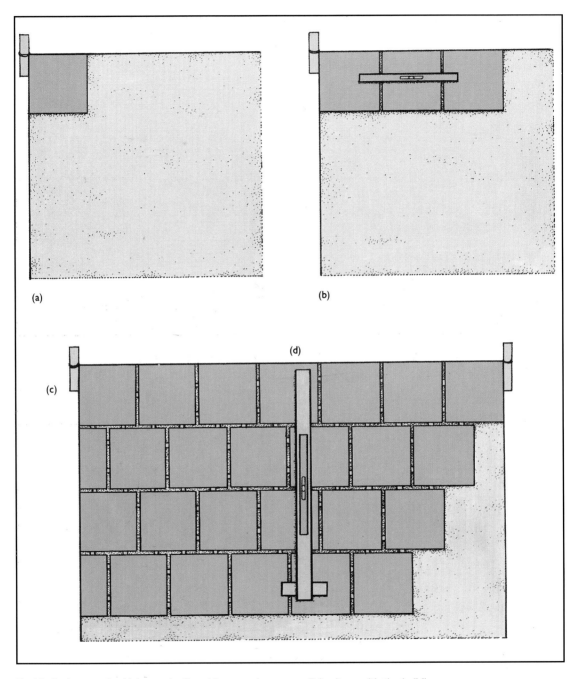

*Fig 89  Laying a patio: (a) lower the first slab on to the mortar, lining it up with the building lines; (b) lay each paving slab next to its neighbour and tap it down, checking the level with a spirit level and leaving a gap in between; (c) use pieces of wood to keep a gap in between the slabs; (d) check fall away from the house with a block cut to the thickness of the fall and a spirit level.*

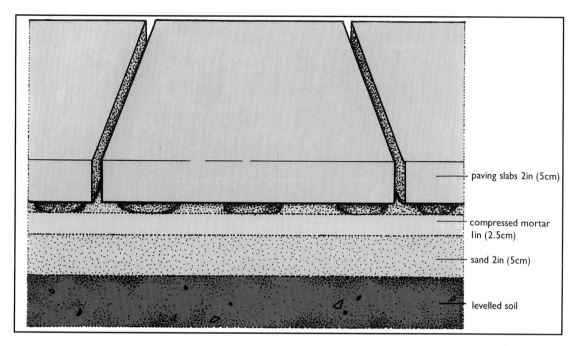

paving slabs 2in (5cm)

compressed mortar
1in (2.5cm)

sand 2in (5cm)

levelled soil

*Fig 90   Shallow sand base. This type of base is normally used only for large stones such as rectangular slabs of concrete or natural stone, or for crazy paving.*

*Fig 91   Hard core and sand base. A deeper base is used for smaller surface units such as bricks or granite setts. Both soil and base must be very well compacted.*

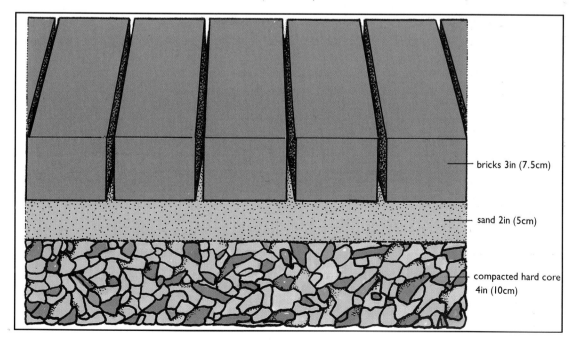

bricks 3in (7.5cm)

sand 2in (5cm)

compacted hard core
4in (10cm)

## CONCRETE MIXES
### (PROPORTIONS BY VOLUME)

| Use | Amounts |
| --- | --- |
| General Purpose (most uses) | 1 part cement 2 parts sand 3 parts 20mm aggregates |
| Foundations | 1 part cement 2½ parts sand 3½ parts 20mm aggregates |
| Paving (drives and other exposed paving) | 1 part cement 1½ parts sand 2½ parts 20mm aggregates |

## MORTAR MIXES
### (PROPORTIONS BY VOLUME)

| Use | Amounts |
| --- | --- |
| Normal | 1 part cement 4½ parts sand |
| Strong | 1 part cement 2½–3½ parts sand |

Fig 92  A watering can fitted with a rose.

to ensure that each piece of stone is well settled into the sand so that the final surface is as level as possible.

For the satisfactory construction of areas using brick-like paviours and granite setts, deeper excavation of the sub-soil is needed and the infilling should be to a greater depth of well compacted hard core or irregularly shaped stone. This is because the bearing surface of each is smaller. The hiring of a plate vibrator is to be recommended for the settling of the hard core and the subsequent settling of the surface finish of bricks or paviours into the course of sharp sand above the hard core.

## Grouting

The open joints between paving slabs need to be grouted with a strong sand and cement mixture. A trowel is used to push the cement well down into the joints to prevent any later shrinkage and cracking. Any cement smears should be wiped off the surface as you work.

A dry mixture of sand and cement may be used, brushed well over the surface, and tamped well into the joints between the slabs with a small stick. This should then be thoroughly moistened, using a watering can fitted with a fine rose.

For paths to be used, they obviously have to be constructed where they are needed. In general, they run between doors, gates and other points of access, to the patio, washing line, shed or greenhouse, but this does not mean that paths have to be in a straight line from A to B. Bear in mind, paths that have curves are softer and more pleasing to the eye, and just as practical.

## Tools

A sound and heavy hammer, a mallet, shovel, rake, builder's tape-measure, a pointing trowel and bricklayer's trowel, a suitable-sized sheet of thick plywood as a mixing board, a square for checking right-angles, a straight edge of timber approximately 6ft (2m) long and a spirit level.

Your builder's merchant or garden centre will supply an all-in aggregate mix, containing aggregate and the correct amount of cement. You will also need a base material of hoggin (a

*Fig 93  A gravel pathway in which self-sown seedlings of* Alchemilla mollis *have been allowed to remain, providing an effect seldom achieved by designed planting.*

sand/gravel mixture) or crushed quarry stone. The builder's merchant will advise you how much material of each you will require if you give him the details of the project with the square yardage (or metric) measurements.

Many of the paving manufacturers produce excellent broadsheets or booklets with step-by-step guides. These can be obtained from the builder's merchant or garden centre.

# CHAPTER 8

# Conservation: The Green Scene

Much is written today about the environment, and we are all being urged to reconsider our accepted practices in the garden as well as in our day-to-day lives. We are using up our natural resources and damaging the atmosphere at a rapid rate. Even water, which is taken so much for granted, is a precious commodity and our use of it will be more expensive in the future.

As a medium for growing plants, we are asked to find suitable alternatives for peat. Peat is cut from blanket bogs, which support a wide range of plant and animal life and are a limited resource.

The home gardener is encouraged to read the labels on herbicides and fertilizers and only use them in the dilutions recommended by the manufacturer. Making up solutions in double strength does not make plants grow more quickly or kill weeds at a faster rate. Several branded mixtures have been banned in the U.K. as experience and research have shown that these particular products become cumulative in the soil to the point where they enter the food chain and are harmful to birds, mammals and man. Fertilizers, in particular nitrates, used by farmers to increase crop yield, are causing contamination of drinking water in some areas, and use of these will have to be severely curtailed.

There are EEC International 'Codes of Conduct' and recommendations which have been drawn up for the future benefit of mankind. It is up to us to do what we can to help the situation by acting responsibly with the products which we use.

## HERBICIDES AND FERTILIZERS

Products are being formulated which, whilst still effective against unwanted plants and insects, are not toxic to human life and which break down readily in the soil. Modern herbicides in the 1940s were based upon phonoxyacetic acids which were found to be useful in the selective control of broad-leaved weeds. These chemicals are closely related to natural plant growth-regulators and are known as hormone weed-killers. These new organic herbicides were revolutionary as very small quantities per acre were effective, compared with the agricultural use of arsenic trioxide in vast quantities per acre.

Most of the mixtures today are made to be biodegradable in the soil, having no long-term residual effect. In response to a demand for 'green' products which are 'environmentally friendly', manufacturers have reverted back to the old soaps and fatty-acid blends used many years ago to control insect problems on plants.

Crop breeders are starting to breed and experiment genetically with plants that will crop well without the need for excessive use of fertilizers such as nitrates, which can leak into the water supply.

## PEAT

For many years, peatlands have been drained to enable these rich, upper soil and peat deposits to be put into cultivation. The peat was extracted

*Fig 94 The white flowered form of* Fritillaria meleagris, *a good spring bulb to grow with ground cover plants.*

as it was regarded as the ideal medium in which to grow plants. Conservationists are now very concerned about this practice as we are depleting these peat deposits to an alarming degree. Peat supplies must be treated in the same way as any other non-renewable resource, and alternatives used as they become available. Manufacturers and producers of potting composts are experimenting with, and to some degree finding success, in alternative mediums that are, in effect, carriers of added fertilizers which nourish the roots and contribute to the well-being of plants. These mixtures are, in the main, using waste products from various industries.

Not least among these waste products is sterilized household refuse that has had all plastic, glass and metals removed. Others include chopped coconut fibre from the husk of the coconut; mixes of animal manure with straw; chopped cocoa bean husks, chopped and fermented sisal; and the fibres of sugar cane after the extraction of sugar. Almost all these waste products have, in the past, been burnt or otherwise destroyed as waste and thought of as being of no commercial value.

## WATER

In the event of long hot summers, it is very difficult to look after our gardens, lawns and plants so that they do not suffer from lack of water.

For example, lawns benefit from infrequent but thorough watering. Grass should not be watered unless it is absolutely essential. If lawns are watered too often, the grass may be weakened and frequent shallow watering only encourages the roots of the grass to seek the surface. If you feel that watering is necessary, this should be carried out in the coolest part of the day and the grass should be thoroughly soaked. The grass roots then seek the moisture in deeper soil, resulting in more resilient plants. Even in the hottest weather, lawns should not be watered more than twice a week.

To keep your lawn looking good in dry periods, let the grass grow a little longer. This way it will stay greener than one that is closely mown. Cutting little but often, trimming the grass to no less than 1¼in (3cm), will act on the grass plants like pruning. This will make the plants more bushy and produce a dense and springy lawn.

Over-watering is often bad for garden plants and can even break down the structure of the soil. To help the soil to retain moisture, dig in manure or compost. When a hole is dug for a new plant or shrub, water the plant well so that the roots get enough moisture to become established. Once the plant or seedlings have taken root and started to grow, they need much less water. Frequent watering simply encourages shallow roots, weakening the plant's resistance to dry conditions. It is best to water in the coolest part of the day and give the plants a thorough soaking.

Plants such as tomatoes need a plentiful supply of water when they are producing fruit. However, shrubs and trees need less, and can suffer from over-watering. Trees, as a general rule being deeper rooted, seldom need watering, but shrubs may need some water during long spells of hot, dry weather.

Hoeing can help by removing weeds that are using up valuable water. It can reduce water loss from the soil surface and stimulate plant growth. Gardens that have plantings of ground cover will lose water less quickly as sun and dry conditions cannot then evaporate moisture from the soil. If there is little ground cover in your garden, then mulching will help considerably. Add a layer of organic material, such as tree bark or compost to keep the sun off the soil. Gravel or pebbles can also help to prevent evaporation of moisture. Polythene mulching mats can be placed around young trees and shrubs and covered with tree bark. These will blend well with the surroundings and be hardly noticeable.

Some plants need much less water than others. Herbs such as lavender, rosemary, thyme and sage for example, need very little water. As many herbs originate from Mediterranean

*Fig 95   A hot scene of flower colour contrasting with the cool swimming pool area.*

*Fig 96  A small knot garden.*

countries, they are accustomed to long, hot summers with very little rain. Watering only lessens their flavour and scent.

Plants in pots can lose moisture very quickly, the pots become heated with the sun and bake, thus losing the moisture from the soil and damaging the plant's roots. Group pots together and keep them shaded, this will help to conserve moisture. Houseplants too, will benefit from this grouping and will need less water. If you are going away for any length of time, place the plants on a tray of moist gravel or a capillary watering mat. These are readily available from garden centres.

Ideally, a rain-water tub is well worth the investment. It will collect the water that runs off the roof of your garden shed or other outbuildings. Rain-water is often a better choice for your garden than tap water, particularly if you live in a hard-water area. Azaleas and rhododendrons in particular, hate lime and suffer when given hard water or when planted in lime-rich soils.

Build up your soil's ability to retain water and accustom your plants to infrequent but thorough watering. Make sure that you are not giving some species more water than they require. A garden with healthy plants that can survive hot, dry weather will reward you if these guide-lines are followed.

# Appendices

## I INSURANCE: ANOTHER ASPECT OF GROUND COVER

Comprehensive home insurance does not generally include the plants in your garden. If you have some valuable terrace pots containing large, mature plants that would possibly be expensive to replace, some insurance companies will provide insurance cover if specifically asked to do so. This is particularly worth while for those with vulnerable front gardens with treasured urns and tubs. Apparently in some of our larger cities, there is a growing problem of theft of such items from privately owned property. It probably does not occur to most people to wonder whether their household contents policy covers the theft of unsecured plants and containers from exposed front steps. It would be worth checking this point with your insurers to find out whether your household policy covers plants lost from the

*Fig 97    A well-executed courtyard planting with low ground cover.*

*Fig 98   A delicate, posy-like combination of colours, backed by a variegated* Elaeagnus.

garden through theft, and those which may be in valuable containers and are within the boundary of the land upon which your house is built.

The usual rule is that you cannot claim for plants that are dug up from your garden, nor for trees and plants that are damaged in a storm, but you may be covered for the theft or destruction of plants that are kept outside your house, conservatory or locked garden shed. Plants, when small, might cost relatively little, but if they have grown to a handsome size in their containers, they might then cost a great deal to replace. However, if you have a household contents policy that includes the phrase 'new for old', you could probably claim for the cost of replacing the grown plant and not the small one that was originally purchased.

It is also worth noting that house policies do not, as a general rule, cover damaged or blown-down fences, gates, shrubs and trees. However, most insurers will pay for the cutting up and removal of damaged trees and shrubs but not for their replacement. Favourable consideration should be given by them to any structural damage that may have been caused to sheds and outhouses, garages, greenhouses and conservatories. No doubt too, the same consideration would be given to damage to ornate brick structures and valuable terrace pots and statues.

It is wise to realize that if you have such valuable items in your garden, that you should specify these in your policy in the first instance. Your insurance cover will then include their value so that the insurance company, in the event of a claim, can make a favourable settlement.

## II HELPFUL HINTS

• You do not need a large garden to enjoy the pleasure that plants will give you with their foliage and flower.

• Do ensure that plants, newly planted, are well watered, using a watering can fitted with a rose. Continue with a regular watering programme until they are fully established.

• A simple soil-testing kit purchased from the garden centre will help you to establish whether your soil tests to alkaline or acid. Take several soil samples from various parts of the garden.

• Whatever your soil and microclimate, set out to make the best of the situation with the many plants that are available. Do not try to fight nature.

• When purchasing plants from nurseries or garden centres, read the labels carefully – many of the pre-printed coloured labels often have good advice on their cultivation.

Prior to planting, do ensure that the plants are free from soil-borne pests that are harmful to the success of the plant's ultimate growth.

• There is no doubt that, in the parts of the garden where there is close growing ground cover, the plants virtually take care of themselves. They will work for you all day long and need the minimum of attention, yet they provide great visual pleasure from both colour and form. Many are, in one sense, trouble-free foliage plants.

*Fig 99* Salvia officinalis *'Icterina' treated as ground cover.*

122

*Fig 100   A massed planting of flowering bulbs used to good effect as seasonal ground cover.*

• Propagation will increase your stock of plants and will enable you to exchange plants with others to obtain a selection and variety.

Ivies, for example, will root at any time of the year, but are best propagated in the growing season. Most ivies are easy to propagate, they may be rooted in the garden, in a cold frame, in a vase of water or in an indoor propagating frame. A compost of peat and sand, soiless compost such as John Innes No. 1 will be suitable. Perlite is another material which may be used alone or mixed with peat. A difficult or precious ivy may be propagated by layering a growth into another pot set alongside. The layer is not cut free until the new roots are established. This practice of layering may also be carried out in the garden.

• Ground cover plants need not be boring. Whilst they cover the soil and minimize weed growth with its inevitable labour intensity, you need never retain a plant in your garden that you do not like.

• A well-designed garden should look good 365 days a year and a gardener should never be a slave to it.

• The best time for planting can well be late spring or early autumn, if your plants have been grown in pots or black polythene bags, as is the trend today in almost all garden centres and nurseries.

Spring plantings are best for those plants described as tender or needing sheltered conditions, and those grey and silver plants with woolly leaves. The same applies to those that need a well-drained soil, so that they are well established before the onset of autumn rains.

123

Deciduous plants, i.e. those that drop their leaves between autumn and spring, can be planted or moved at any time while they are leafless.

• Certain plants will need an occasional tidy up, those that are vigorous and have to be restrained from swamping other plants and those that become straggly and require cutting back to keep them compact, such as the heaths and heathers and many of the grey and silver plants. It will also be necessary to remove dead twigs, old flowering stems and, with some of the woody plants, pruning may be necessary in the early years after planting, to encourage branching near ground level.

• The herbaceous plants, i.e. those that die down in the winter and are clump forming, will want dividing, probably every 4–5 years. They tend to become overcrowded with the centre of the clumps dying back and becoming unsightly and less productive.

• There are 12,000 or more species of plants that are readily available to choose from. Garden designers have been encouraging us to think in terms of pavings, steps, arches, brick circles, reproduction statues and an array of classical urns, but it would seem that we need a shift in direction towards plants and away from ornamentation. A garden that is full of plants is surely a more enjoyable solution that putting it all or most of it under paving stones in the quest for a 'low maintenance' garden.

• Visit other people's gardens and discover how plants behave 'in action'. This way, ideas for planting and plant combinations can be gleaned. This can be a good way of solving the dilemma facing many people when looking at their gardens with a view to planting and a way of facing the first step forward from good intentions to effective action.

## III GLOSSARY

**Acute**  Sharply pointed, not drawn out.
**Adventitious**  Roots arising from points of the plant other than the seed. Usually implies roots on aerial stems.
**Aerial root**  A root originating above ground.
**Anther**  Pollen-bearing part of the stamen.
**Apex**  The tip of a frond or pinna.
**Aphis**  The scientific name for aphids, a common insect pest. Their food is obtained by sucking the juices of the plant.
**Axil**  Angle formed by a leaf or lateral branch with the stem.
**Axis**  The central part of a frond about which the blade is arranged.

**Bicolour**  Having two distinct colours.
**Bipinnate**  When the leaf is pinnate, the divisions are also pinnate.
**Bract**  Modified leaf at the base of a flower stalk or flower cluster.

**Calyx**  Collective term for the flower sepals.
**Cordate**  Heart-shaped.
**Corolla**  Collective term for the flower petals.
**Corymbose**  Tasselled. Bunch crested.
**Cultivar**  Garden variety of a plant of a form found in the wild and maintained in cultivation.

**Deciduous**  With leaves that fall annually, usually in autumn.
**Deltoid**  Shaped like an equilateral triangle.
**Dentate**  Toothed.
**Digitate**  Of crests divided like fingers of a hand.
**Double**  Flowers with more than the usual number of petals.

**Entire**  Undivided, not toothed.
**Evergreen**  Remaining green throughout the winter.

**Family**  Group of genera with important characteristics in common, for example, Rosaceae, the rose family.

*Fig 101* Cyclamen repandum *spreading by self-sown seedlings, flowering profusely in dappled woodland shade.*

**Fastigiate**  With a conical or tapering outline.
**Fungicide**  A chemical used to kill fungi such as mildew, black spot or rust on roses.

**Glaucous**  Having a bluish bloom.
**Glume**  Membraneous or chaff-like scales enclosing the spikelets of a grass or flower of a sedge.

**Heeling in**  Temporary planting before permanent placing.
**Humus**  Organic matter that is well rotted.
**Hybrid**  A cross between different species, sub-species or varieties.

**Insecticide**  Any substance that will kill insects, mites and other pests.

**Lanceolate**  Lance-shaped, tapering to both ends, wider in the lower third.
**Linear**  Several times longer than wide; slender.
**Lobe**  A shallow segment.

**Marginate**  Having a closely frilled margin.
**Mulch**  A dressing of organic matter applied to the surface of the soil to assist its water retention and suppress the growth of annual weeds.

**Node**  The point on a stem where the leaves arise.

**Ovate**  Egg-shaped, the wider part nearer than the attachment.

**Peltate**  Shield-like, with central attachment.

**Petiole**  The stalk by which the leaf is attached to the stem.

**Pinna**  Primary division of a pinnate blade.

**Pinnate**  With leaves arranged on each side of the same stalk.

**Pinnule**  The secondary division in a frond.

**Rachis**  The central axis of a frond excluding the stalk.

**Reflexed**  Bent backwards or downwards.

**Rhizome**  An underground stem, persistent, from which fronds or leaves arise.

**Rhomboid**  A four-sided figure having no right angles; diamond-shaped.

**Sagittate**  Arrow-shaped.

**Segments**  Any division of a leaf blade not reaching the midrib.

**Semi-evergreen**  Losing some or all leaves in severe weather.

**Sessile**  Having no stalk.

**Simple**  Undivided.

**Spent hops**  The residue left from brewing. A good source of organic material.

**Sport**  A mutation arising from genetic changes in a plant or part of a plant. It can cause variation in growth habit or change of leaf colour or flower colour.

**Spur**  A short branch or shoot.

**Stamen**  The pollen-bearing organ of a flower.

**Stipules**  Leaf-like appendages at the base of a flower stalk, usually in pairs.

**Tuber**  A fleshy thickening or outgrowth of an underground stem from which new plants arise. It acts as a storage system.

*Fig 102  A sheltered courtyard area with* Angelica archangelica *in flower on the right, with an original use of the horseradish,* Armoracia rusticana, *together with plantings of clipped Box and tender plants placed in their summer situation.*

# Index